Old Gods

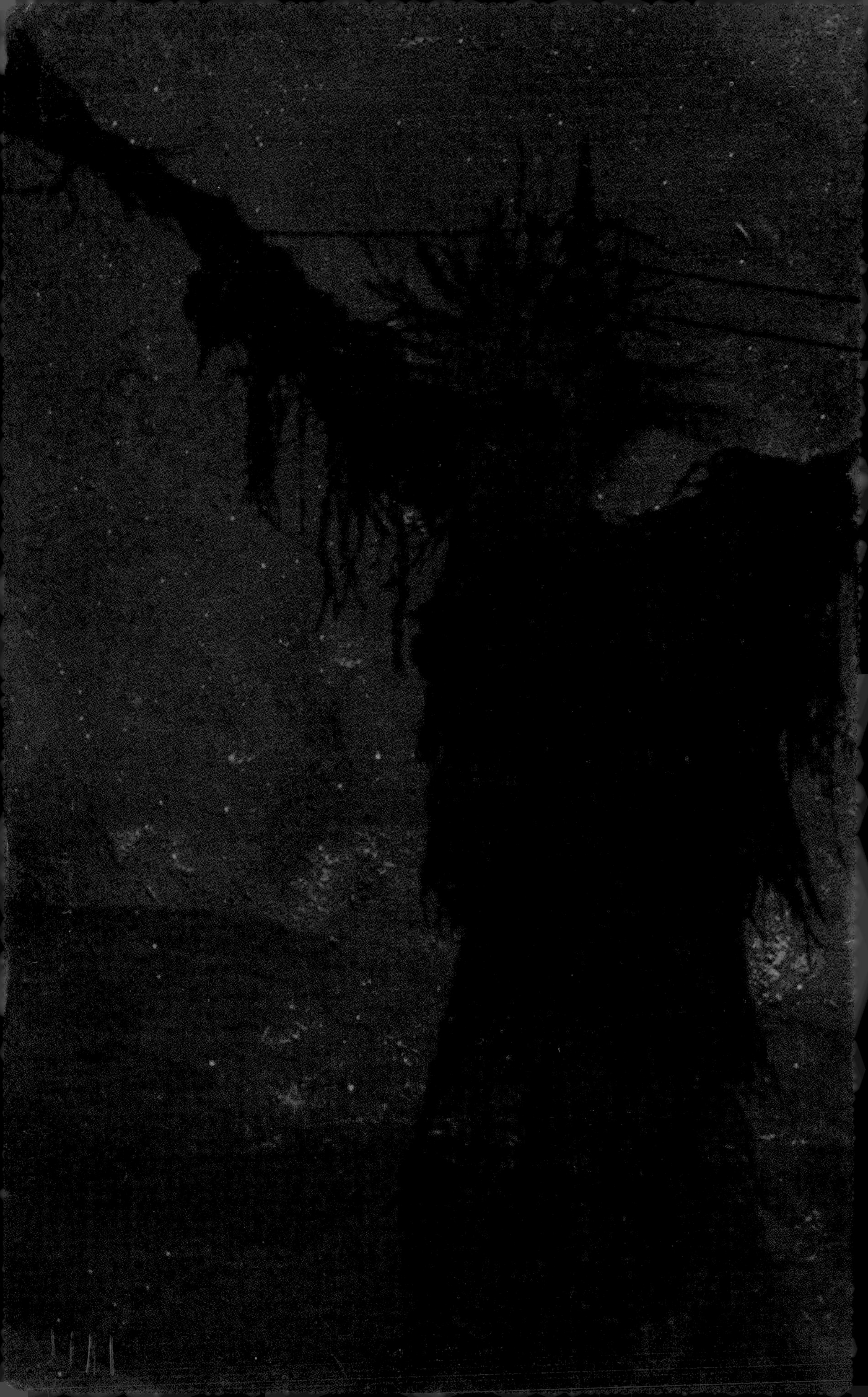

PLANET OF THE APES™

OF THE

Old Gods

2/1/2011

WRITER

IAN EDGINTON

PENCILS

PACO MEDINA
AND **ADRIAN SIBAR**

INKS

NORMAN LEE AND
JUAN VLASCO

COLORS

GUY MAJOR AND
DAN JACKSON

LETTERING

STEVE DUTRO

COVER

**CHRIS BACHALO,
TIM TOWNSEND,
AND BODHI TREE**

DARK HORSE COMICS®

INKING ASSISTANCE
JOE SANCHEZ
MIKE REJES
SANDRA JIMENEZ

ASSISTANT EDITOR
PHILIP SIMON

EDITOR
PHIL AMARA

DESIGNER
DEBRA BAILEY

PUBLISHER
MIKE RICHARDSON

This volume collects issues #1-3 of the comics series

published by
Dark Horse Comics, Inc.
10956 S.E. Main Street
Milwaukie, OR 97222

www.darkhorse.com

To find a comics shop in your area, call the Comic Shop Locator Service toll-free at 1-888-266-4226.

First edition: February 2002
ISBN: 1-56971-668-4

Printed in Canada

10 9 8 7 6 5 4 3 2 1

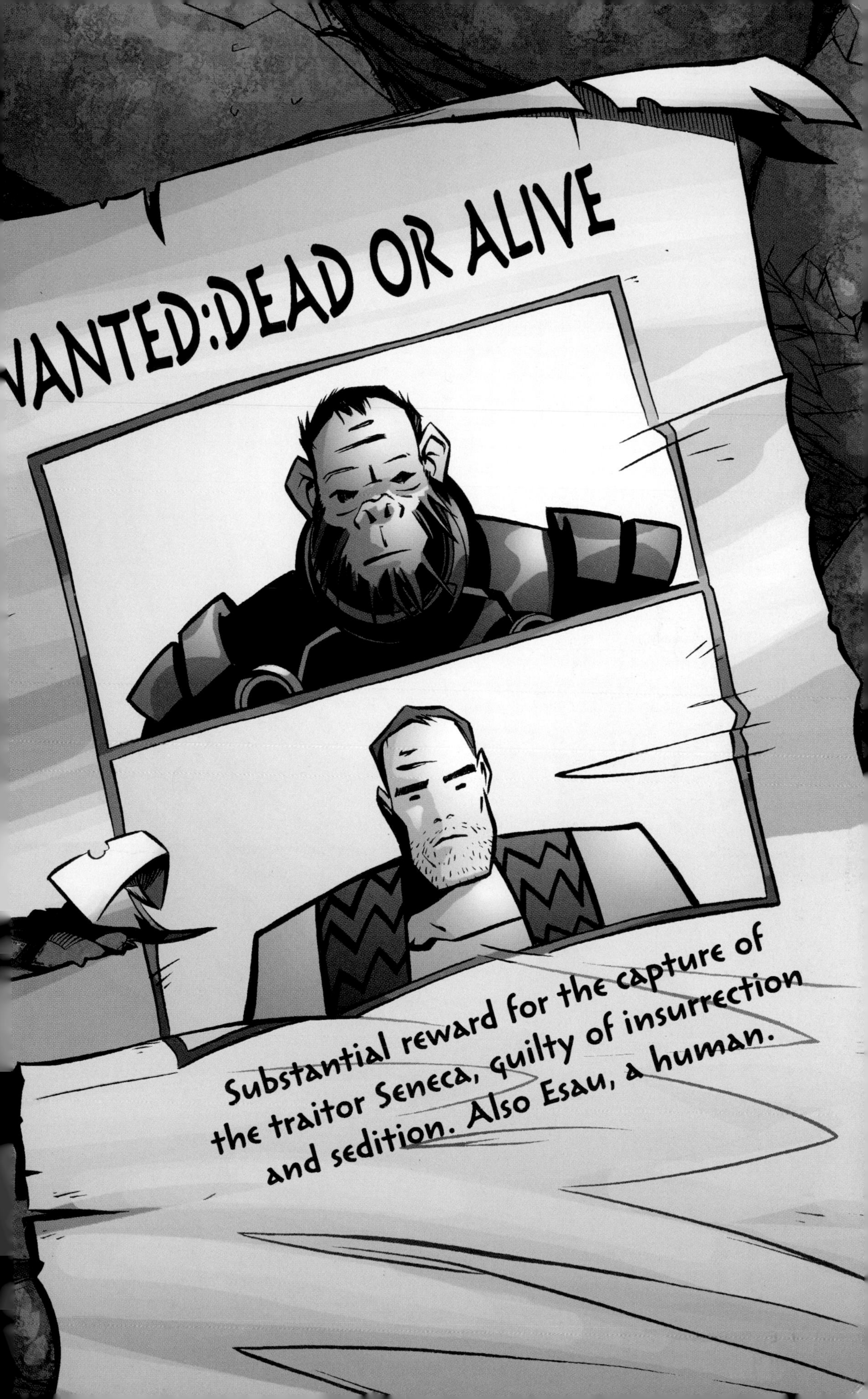
WANTED: DEAD OR ALIVE
Substantial reward for the capture of the traitor Seneca, guilty of insurrection and sedition. Also Esau, a human.

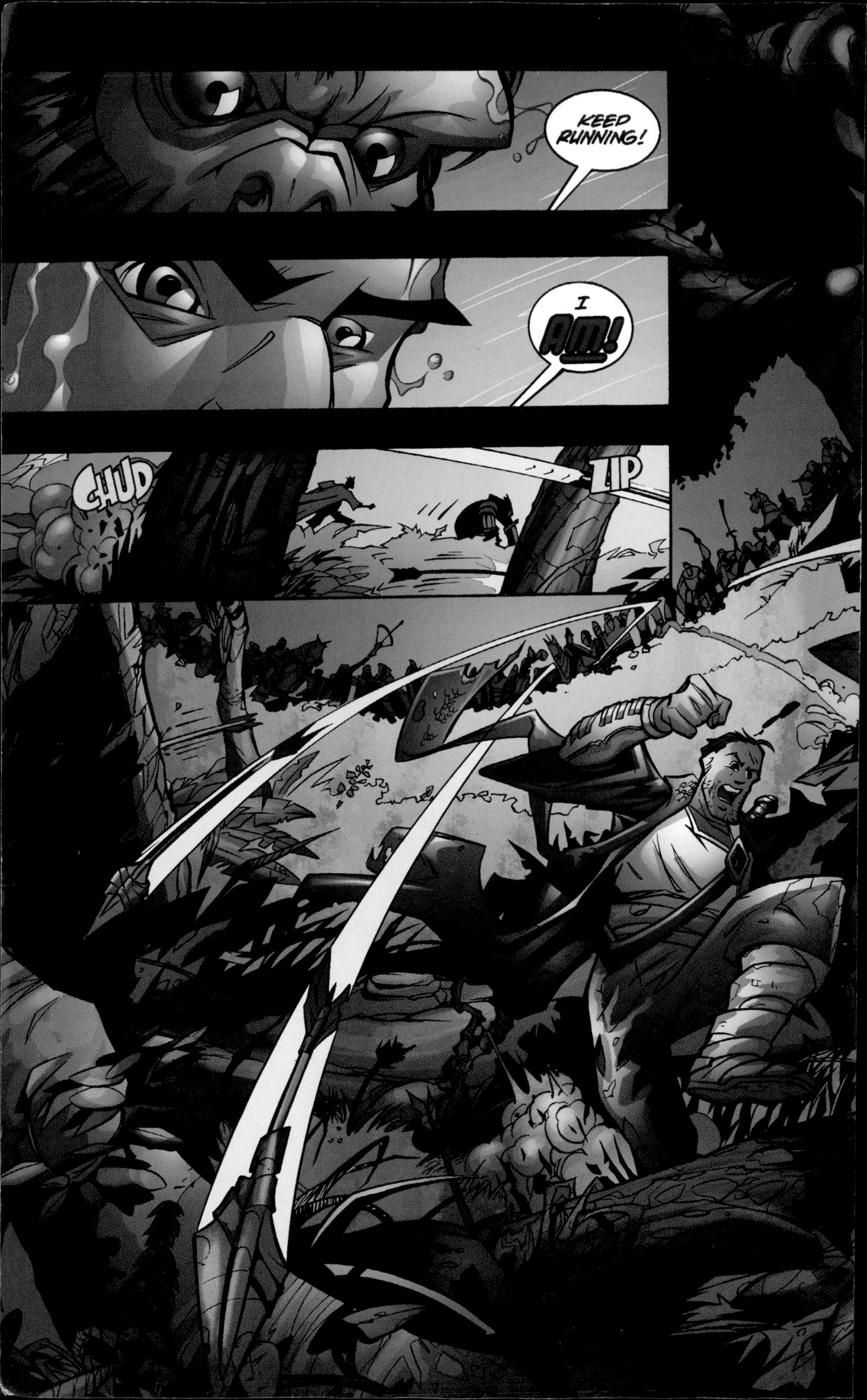
KEEP RUNNING!
I AM!
CHUD
ZIP

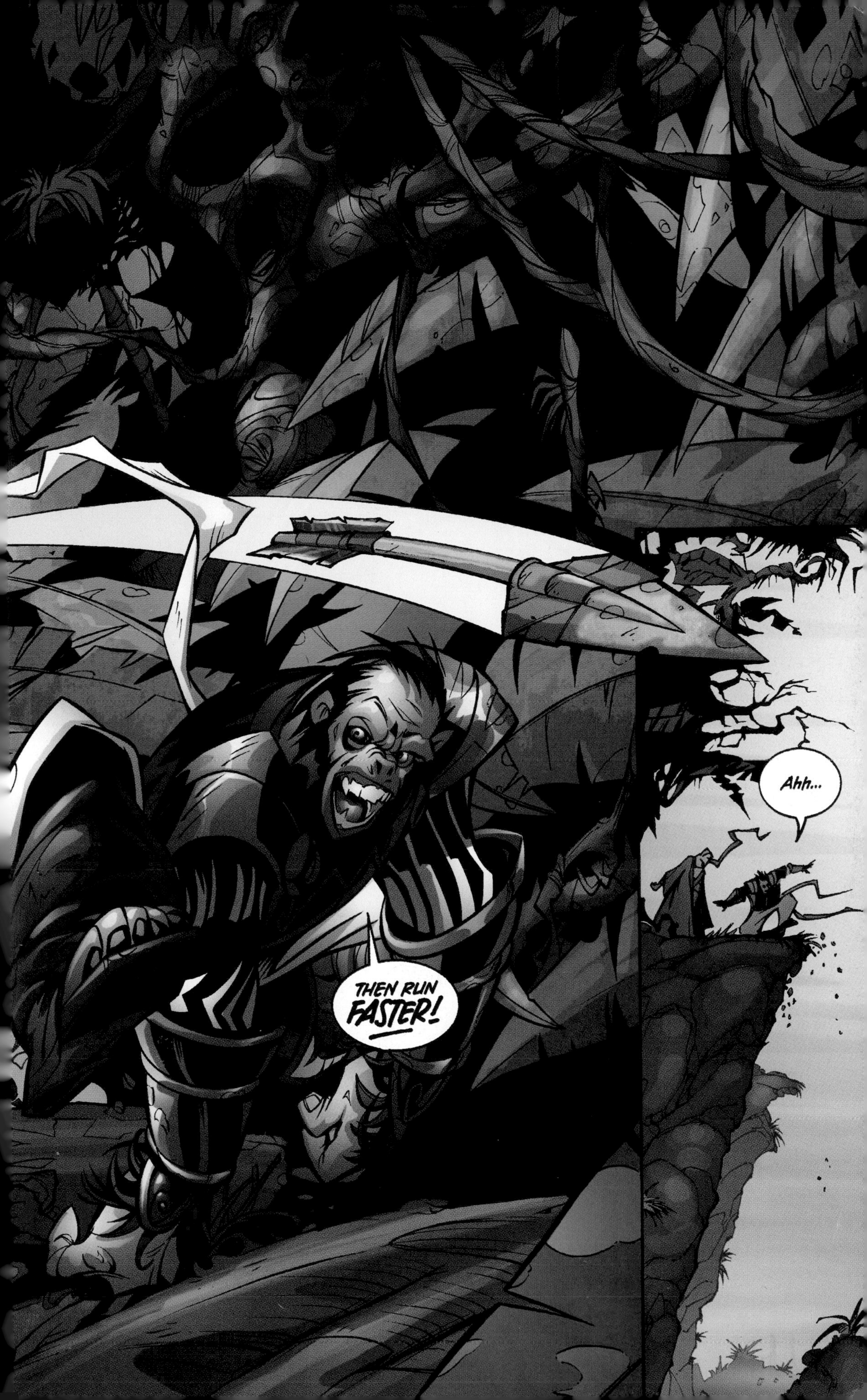
Ahh...
THEN RUN FASTER!

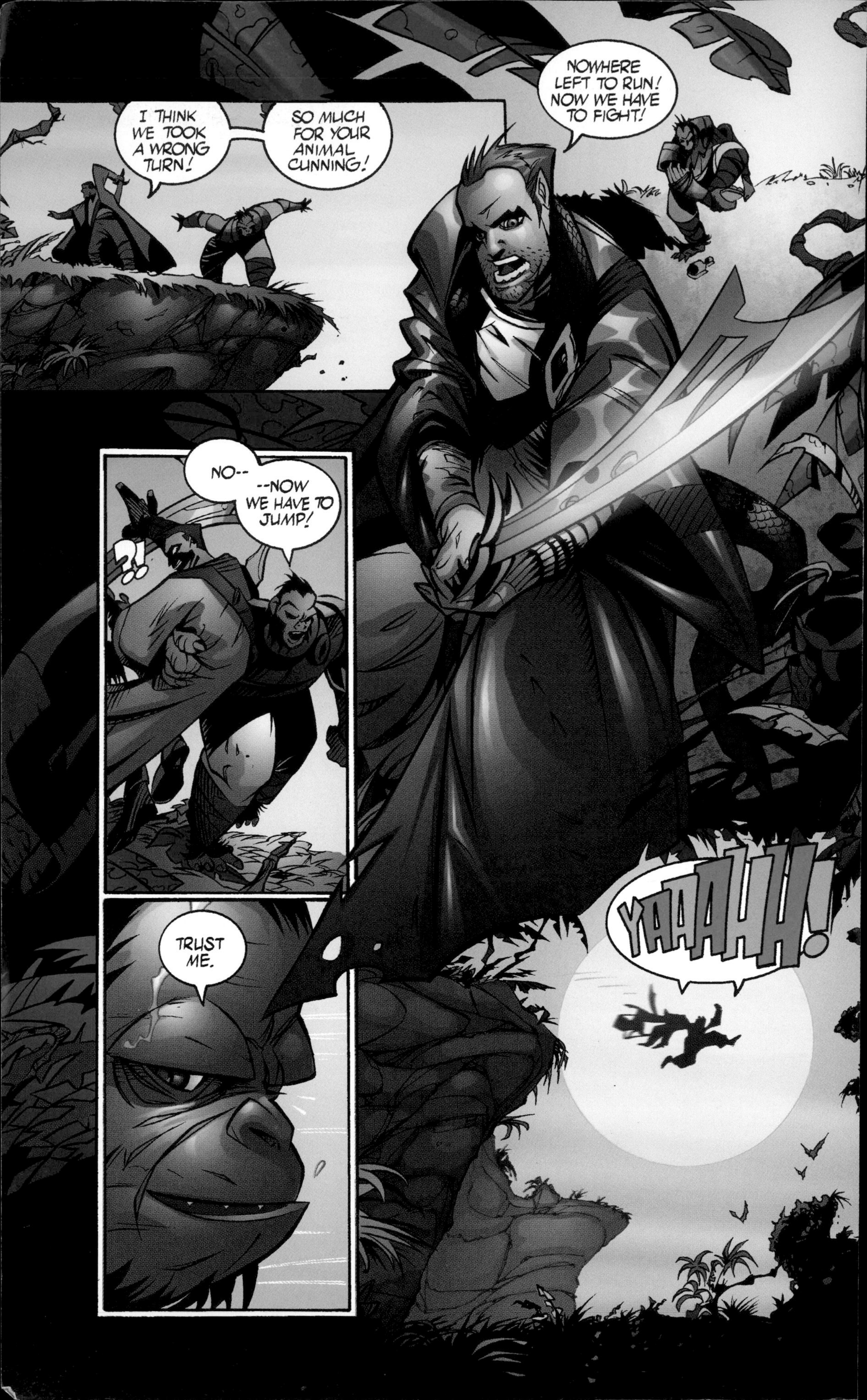
I THINK WE TOOK A WRONG TURN!
SO MUCH FOR YOUR ANIMAL CUNNING!
NOWHERE LEFT TO RUN! NOW WE HAVE TO FIGHT!
NO--
--NOW WE HAVE TO JUMP!
?!
TRUST ME.
YAAAHH!

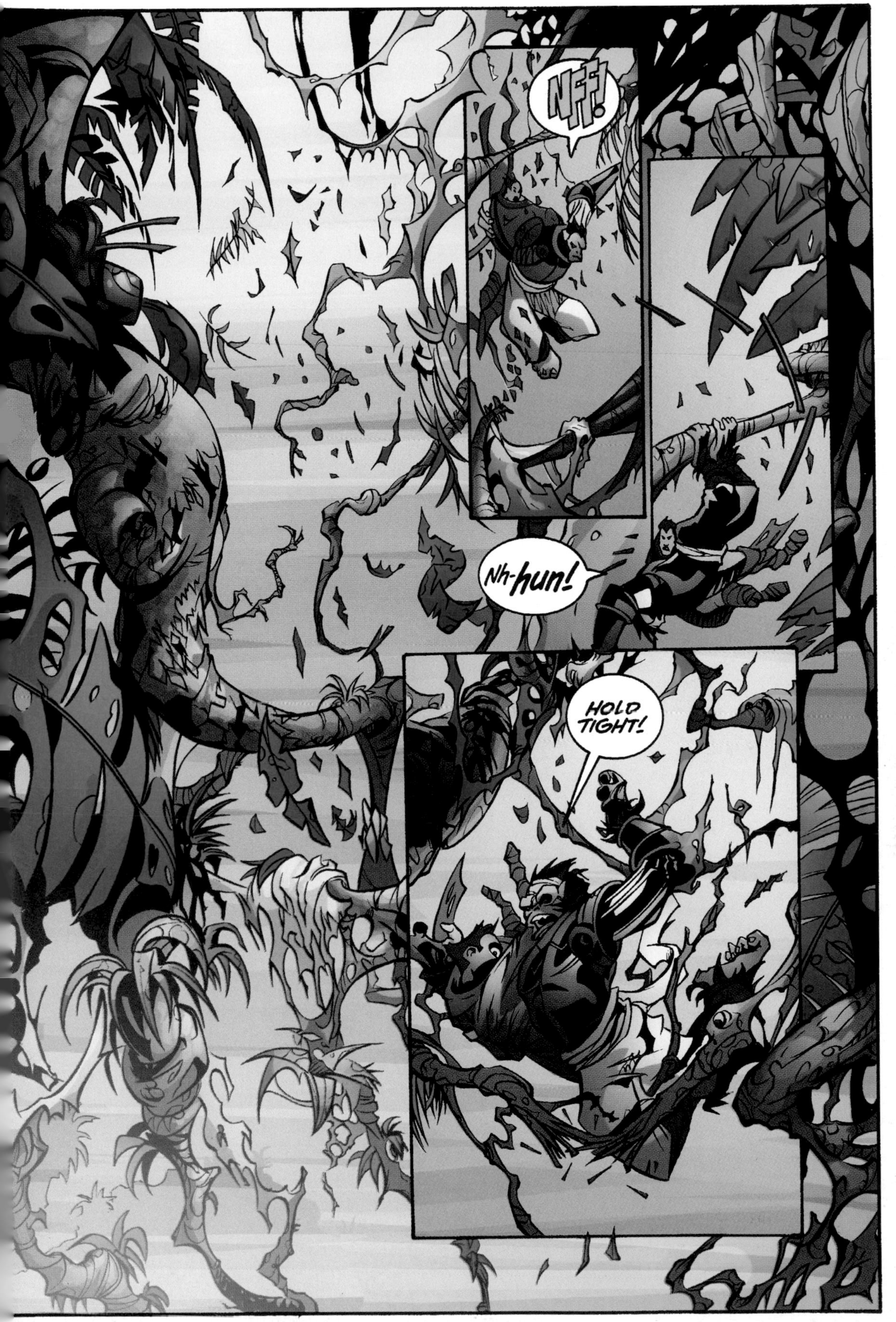
NFF!
Nh-hun!
HOLD TIGHT!

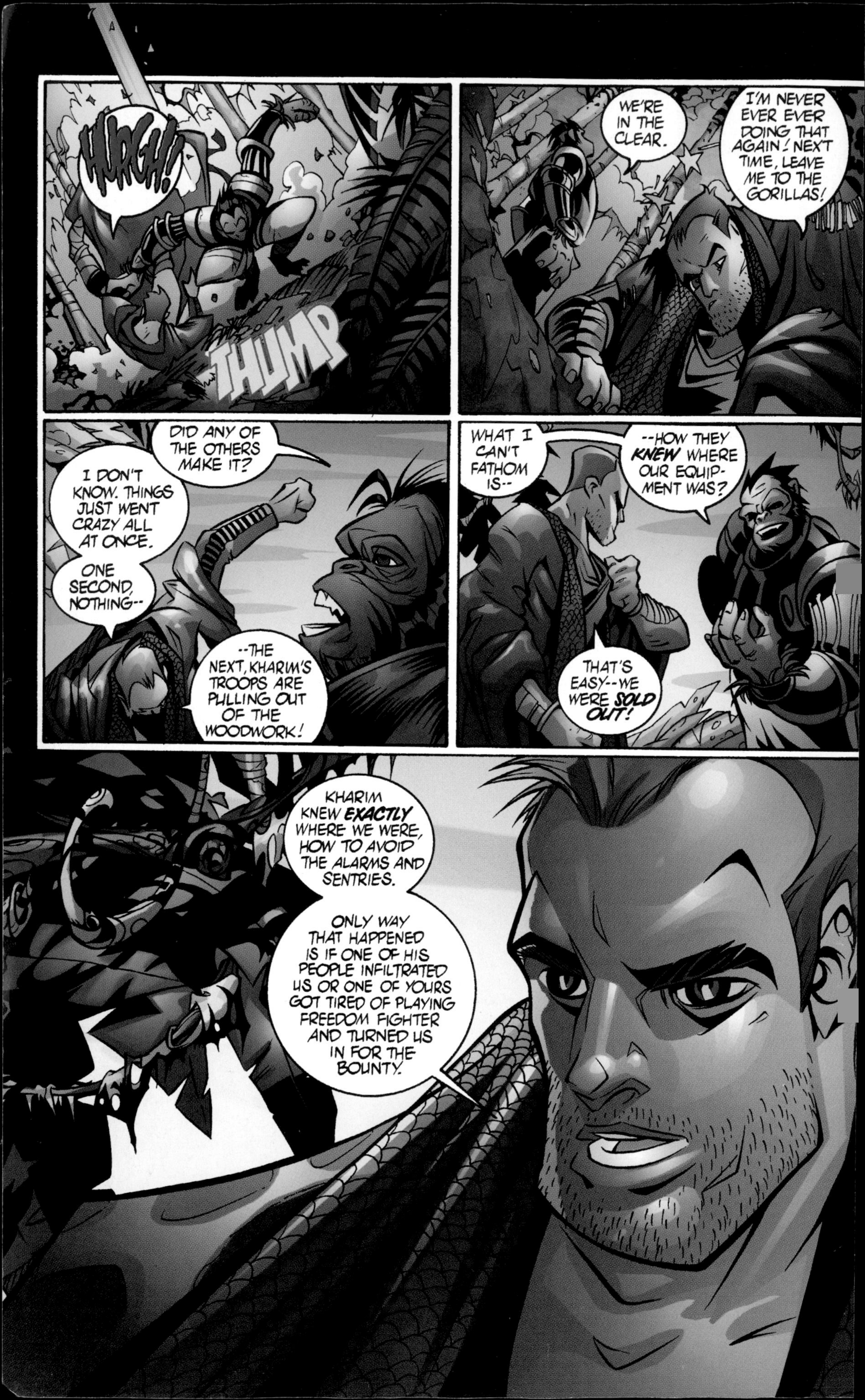
HURGH!
THUMP
WE'RE IN THE CLEAR.
I'M NEVER EVER EVER DOING THAT AGAIN! NEXT TIME, LEAVE ME TO THE GORILLAS!
DID ANY OF THE OTHERS MAKE IT?
I DON'T KNOW. THINGS JUST WENT CRAZY ALL AT ONCE.
ONE SECOND, NOTHING--
--THE NEXT, KHARIM'S TROOPS ARE PULLING OUT OF THE WOODWORK!
WHAT I CAN'T FATHOM IS--
--HOW THEY KNEW WHERE OUR EQUIPMENT WAS?
THAT'S EASY--WE WERE SOLD OUT!
KHARIM KNEW EXACTLY WHERE WE WERE, HOW TO AVOID THE ALARMS AND SENTRIES.
ONLY WAY THAT HAPPENED IS IF ONE OF HIS PEOPLE INFILTRATED US OR ONE OF YOURS GOT TIRED OF PLAYING FREEDOM FIGHTER AND TURNED US IN FOR THE BOUNTY.

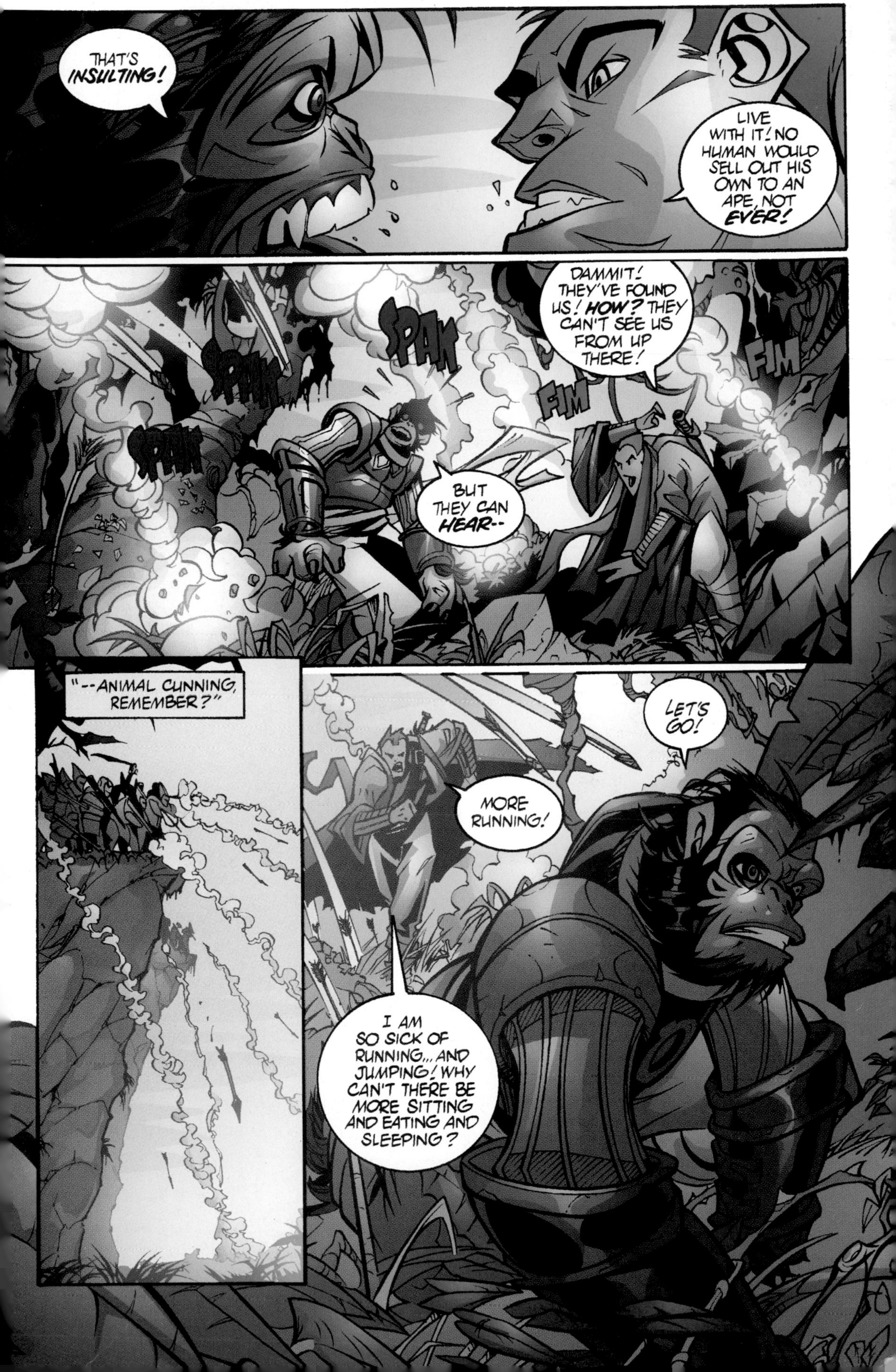
THAT'S INSULTING!
LIVE WITH IT! NO HUMAN WOULD SELL OUT HIS OWN TO AN APE, NOT EVER!
SPAK
SPAK
SPAK
DAMMIT! THEY'VE FOUND US! HOW? THEY CAN'T SEE US FROM UP THERE!
FIM
FIM
BUT THEY CAN HEAR--
"--ANIMAL CUNNING, REMEMBER?"
LET'S GO!
MORE RUNNING!
I AM SO SICK OF RUNNING... AND JUMPING! WHY CAN'T THERE BE MORE SITTING AND EATING AND SLEEPING?

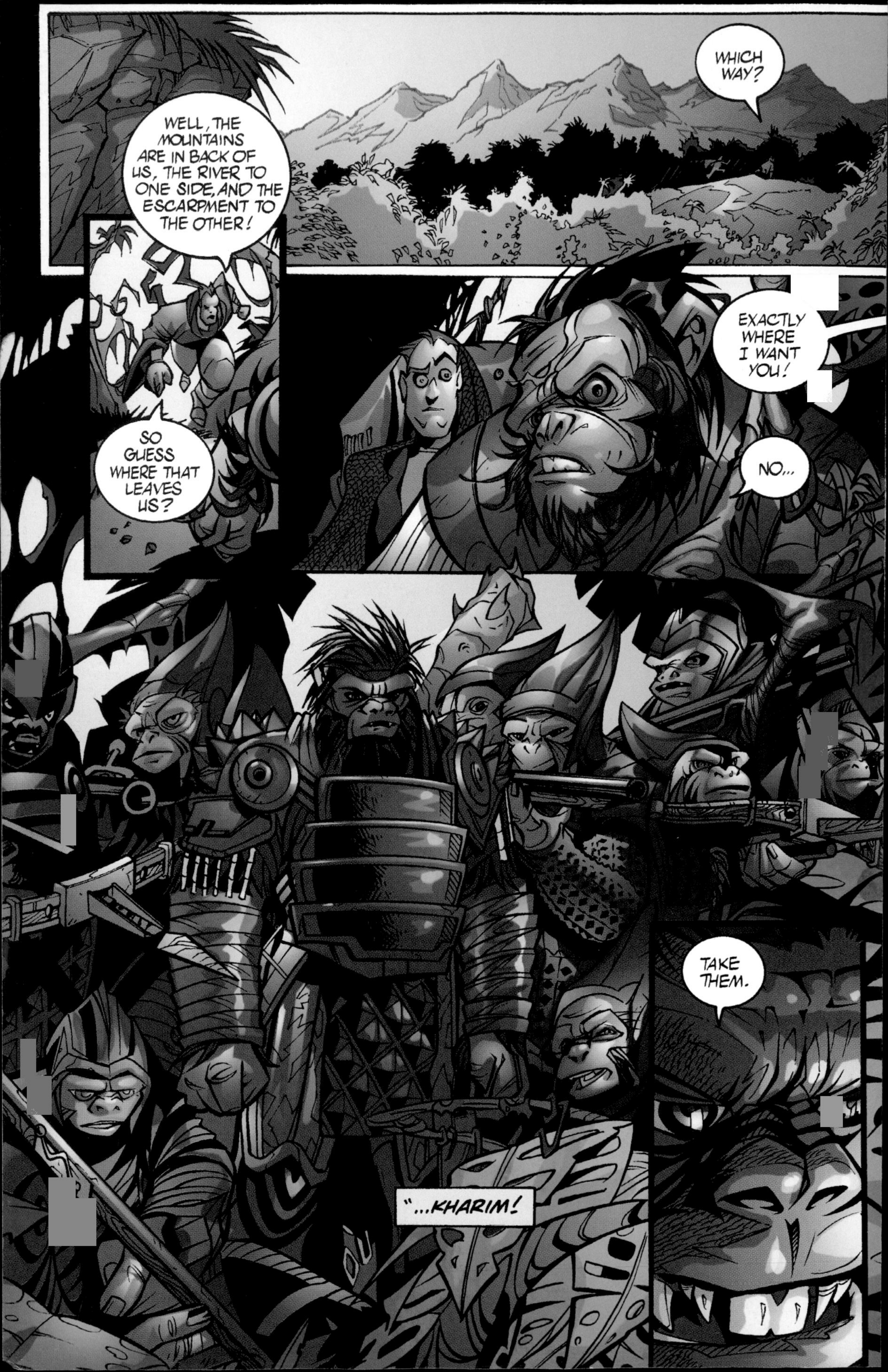
WHICH WAY?
WELL, THE MOUNTAINS ARE IN BACK OF US, THE RIVER TO ONE SIDE, AND THE ESCARPMENT TO THE OTHER!
SO GUESS WHERE THAT LEAVES US?
EXACTLY WHERE I WANT YOU!
NO...
TAKE THEM.
"...KHARIM!

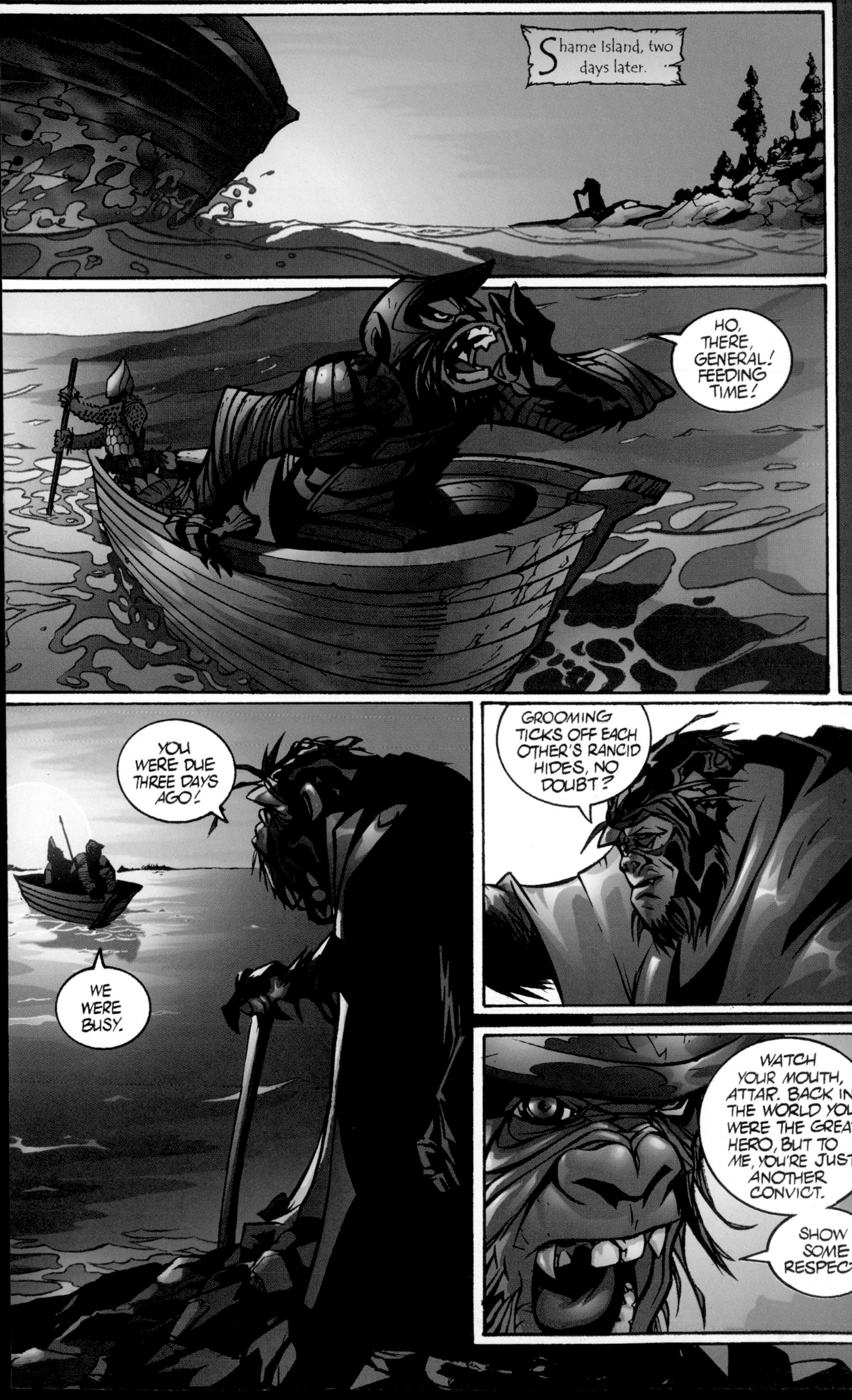
Shame Island, two days later.
HO, THERE, GENERAL! FEEDING TIME!
YOU WERE DUE THREE DAYS AGO!
WE WERE BUSY.
GROOMING TICKS OFF EACH OTHER'S RANCID HIDES, NO DOUBT?
WATCH YOUR MOUTH, ATTAR. BACK IN THE WORLD YOU WERE THE GREAT HERO, BUT TO ME, YOU'RE JUST ANOTHER CONVICT.
SHOW SOME RESPECT.

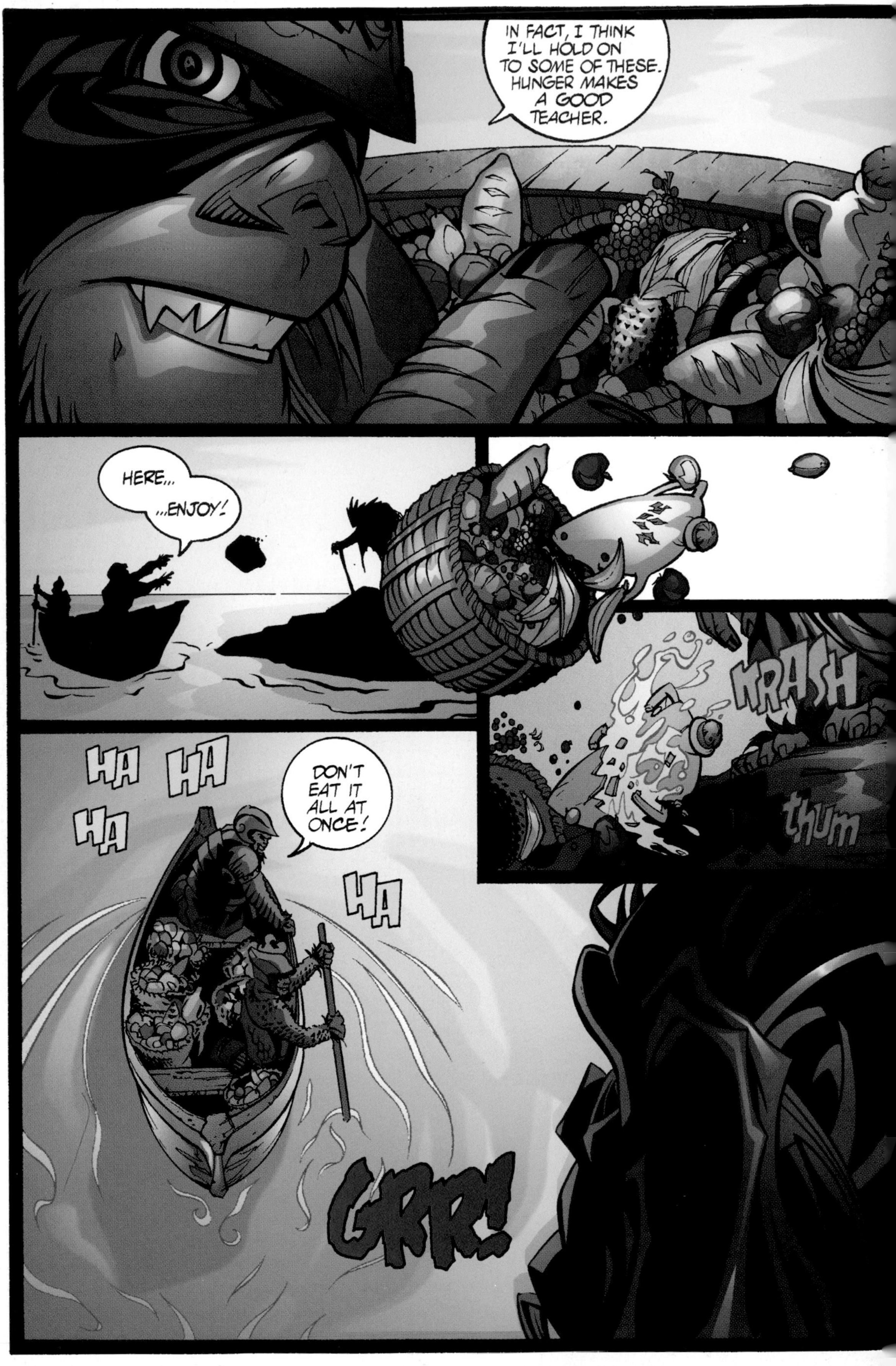
IN FACT, I THINK I'LL HOLD ON TO SOME OF THESE. HUNGER MAKES A GOOD TEACHER.
HERE... ...ENJOY!
KRASH
thum
HA HA HA
DON'T EAT IT ALL AT ONCE!
HA
GRR!

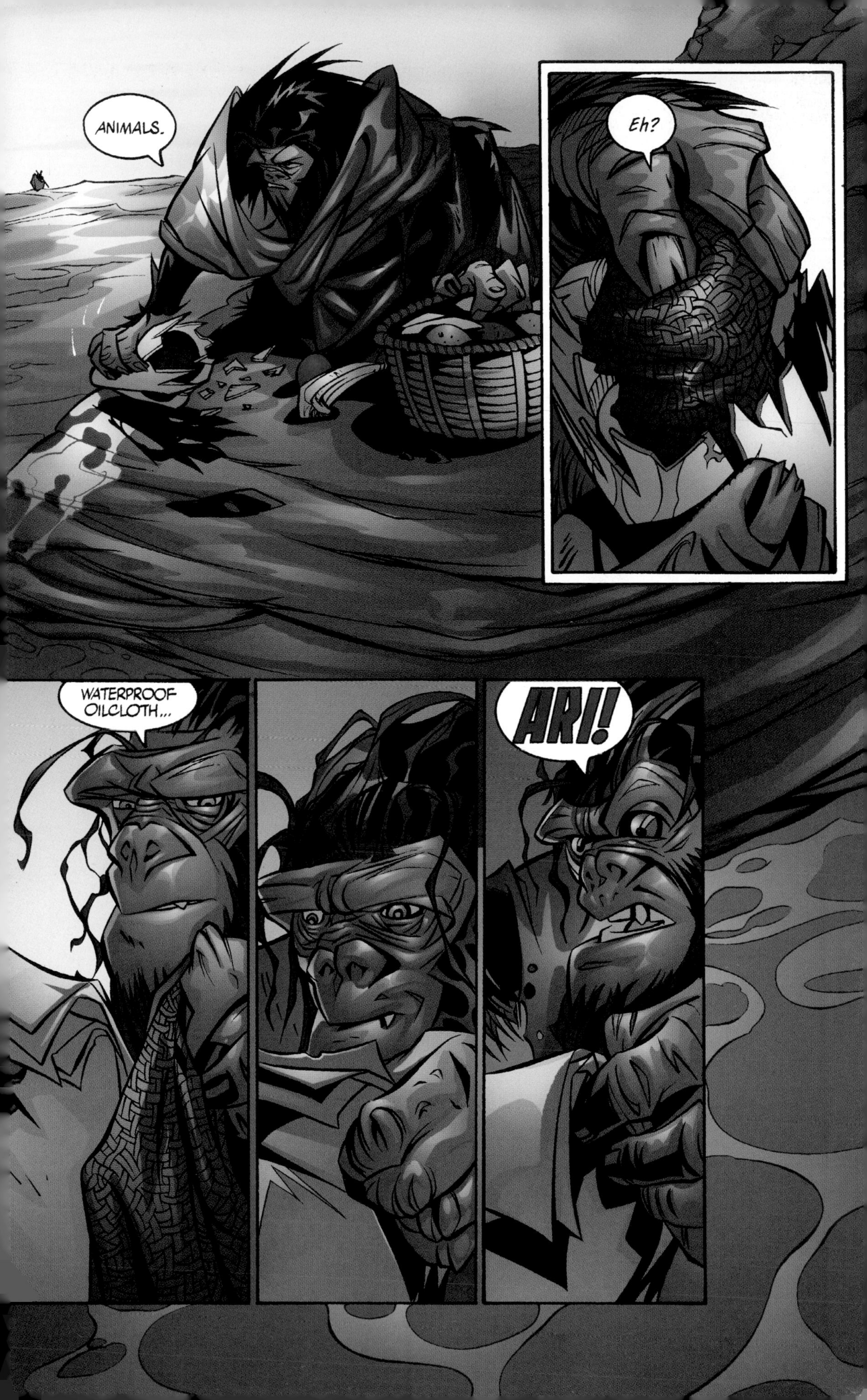
ANIMALS.
Eh?
WATERPROOF OILCLOTH...
ARI!

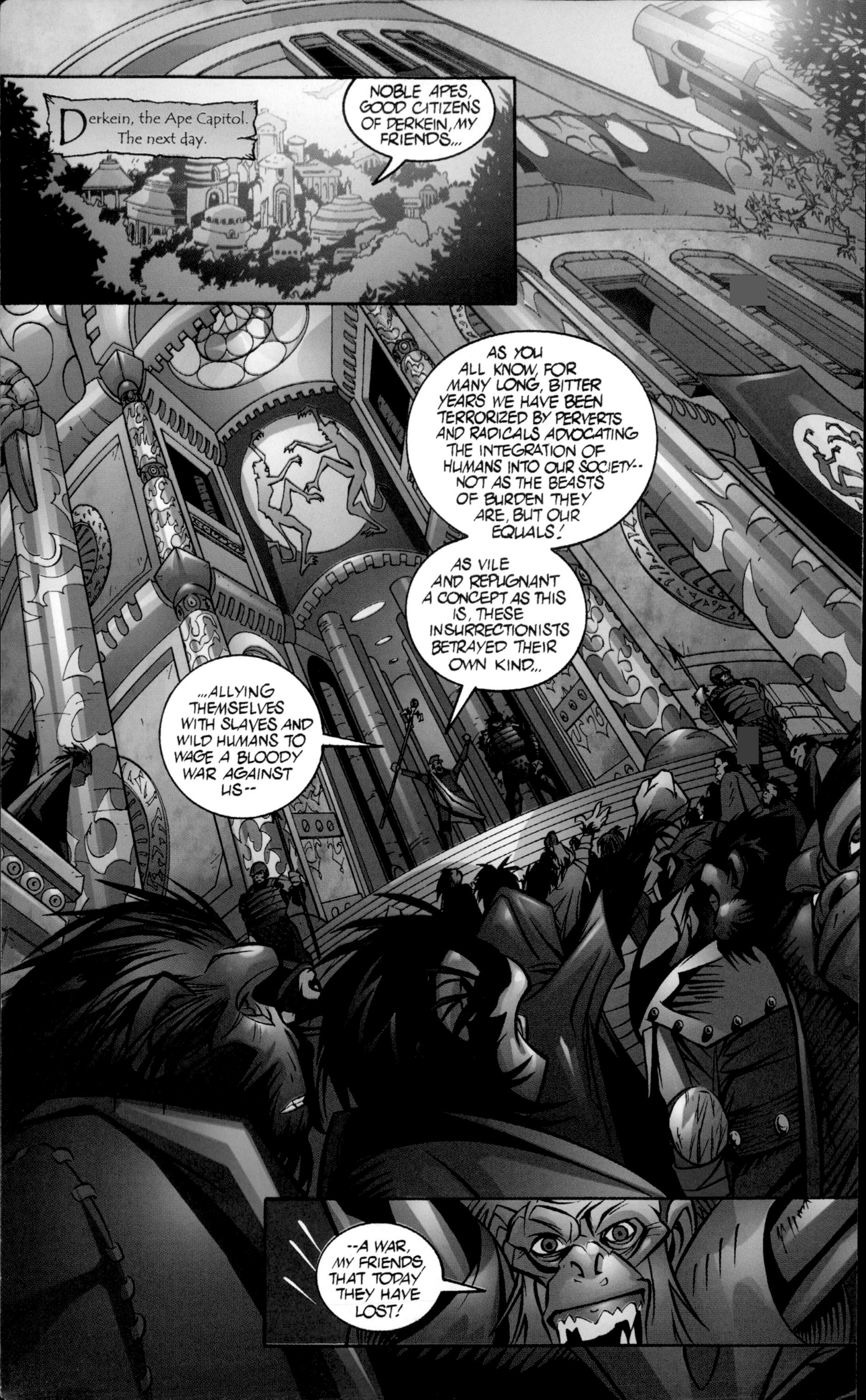
Derkein, the Ape Capitol. The next day.
NOBLE APES, GOOD CITIZENS OF DERKEIN, MY FRIENDS...
AS YOU ALL KNOW, FOR MANY LONG, BITTER YEARS WE HAVE BEEN TERRORIZED BY PERVERTS AND RADICALS ADVOCATING THE INTEGRATION OF HUMANS INTO OUR SOCIETY-- NOT AS THE BEASTS OF BURDEN THEY ARE, BUT OUR EQUALS!
AS VILE AND REPUGNANT A CONCEPT AS THIS IS, THESE INSURRECTIONISTS BETRAYED THEIR OWN KIND...
...ALLYING THEMSELVES WITH SLAVES AND WILD HUMANS TO WAGE A BLOODY WAR AGAINST US--
--A WAR, MY FRIENDS, THAT TODAY THEY HAVE LOST!

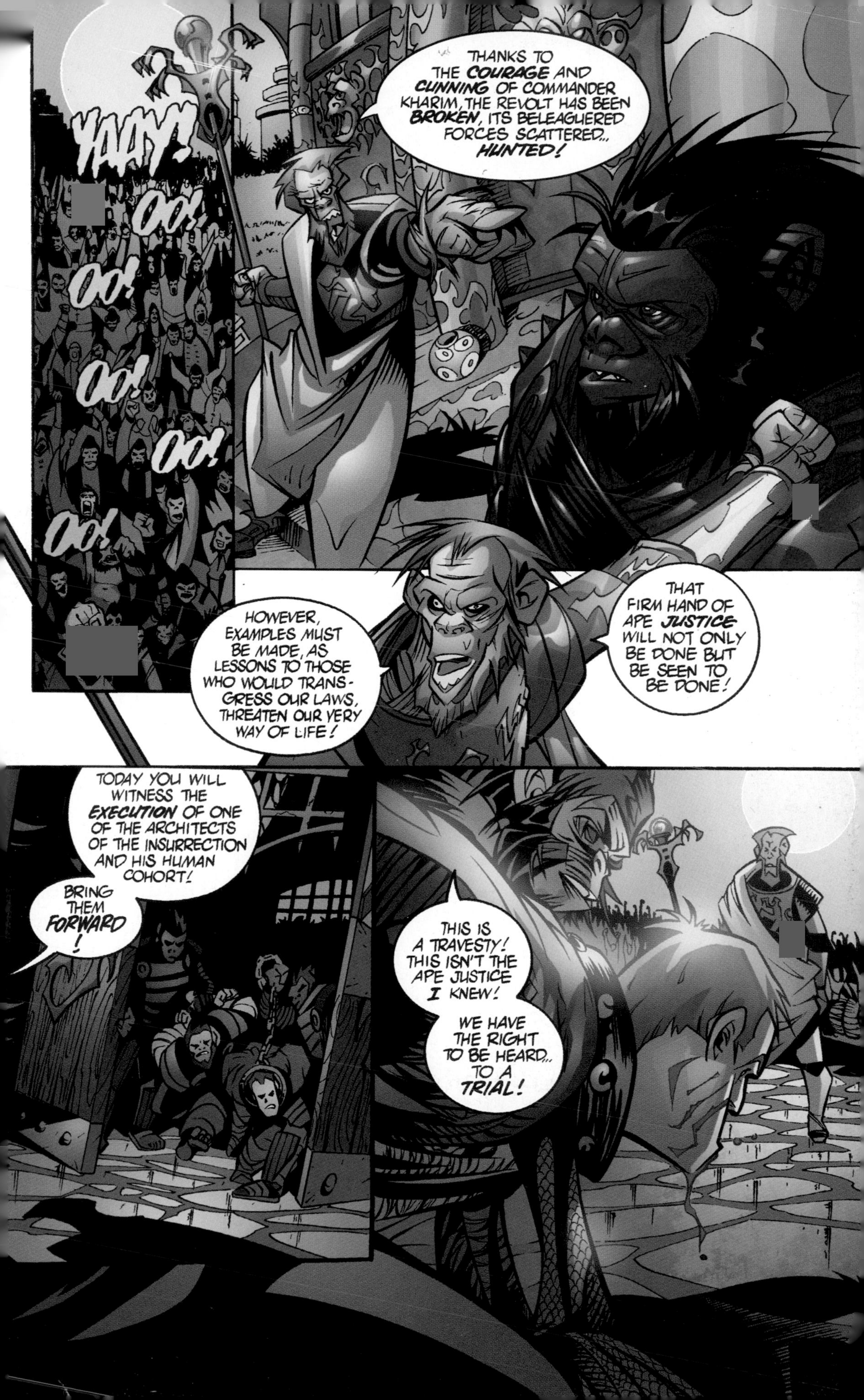
YAAAY!
OO!
OO!
OO!
OO!
OO!
THANKS TO THE COURAGE AND CUNNING OF COMMANDER KHARIM, THE REVOLT HAS BEEN BROKEN, ITS BELEAGUERED FORCES SCATTERED... HUNTED!
HOWEVER, EXAMPLES MUST BE MADE, AS LESSONS TO THOSE WHO WOULD TRANS-GRESS OUR LAWS, THREATEN OUR VERY WAY OF LIFE!
THAT FIRM HAND OF APE JUSTICE WILL NOT ONLY BE DONE BUT BE SEEN TO BE DONE!
TODAY YOU WILL WITNESS THE EXECUTION OF ONE OF THE ARCHITECTS OF THE INSURRECTION AND HIS HUMAN COHORT!
BRING THEM FORWARD!
THIS IS A TRAVESTY! THIS ISN'T THE APE JUSTICE I KNEW!
WE HAVE THE RIGHT TO BE HEARD... TO A TRIAL!

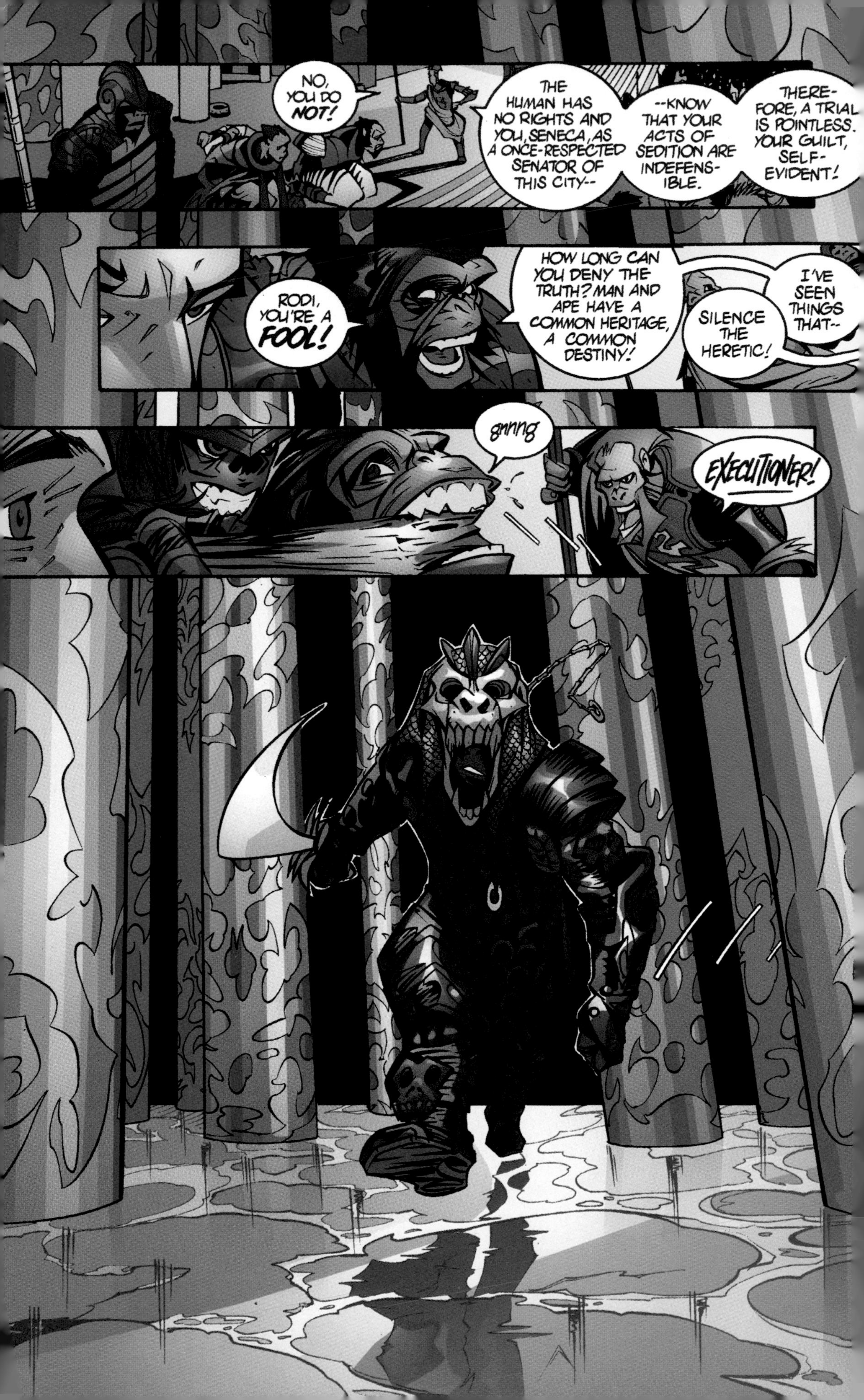
NO, YOU DO NOT!
THE HUMAN HAS NO RIGHTS AND YOU, SENECA, AS A ONCE-RESPECTED SENATOR OF THIS CITY--
--KNOW THAT YOUR ACTS OF SEDITION ARE INDEFENSIBLE.
THEREFORE, A TRIAL IS POINTLESS. YOUR GUILT, SELF-EVIDENT!
RODI, YOU'RE A FOOL!
HOW LONG CAN YOU DENY THE TRUTH? MAN AND APE HAVE A COMMON HERITAGE, A COMMON DESTINY!
I'VE SEEN THINGS THAT--
SILENCE THE HERETIC!
gnnng
EXECUTIONER!

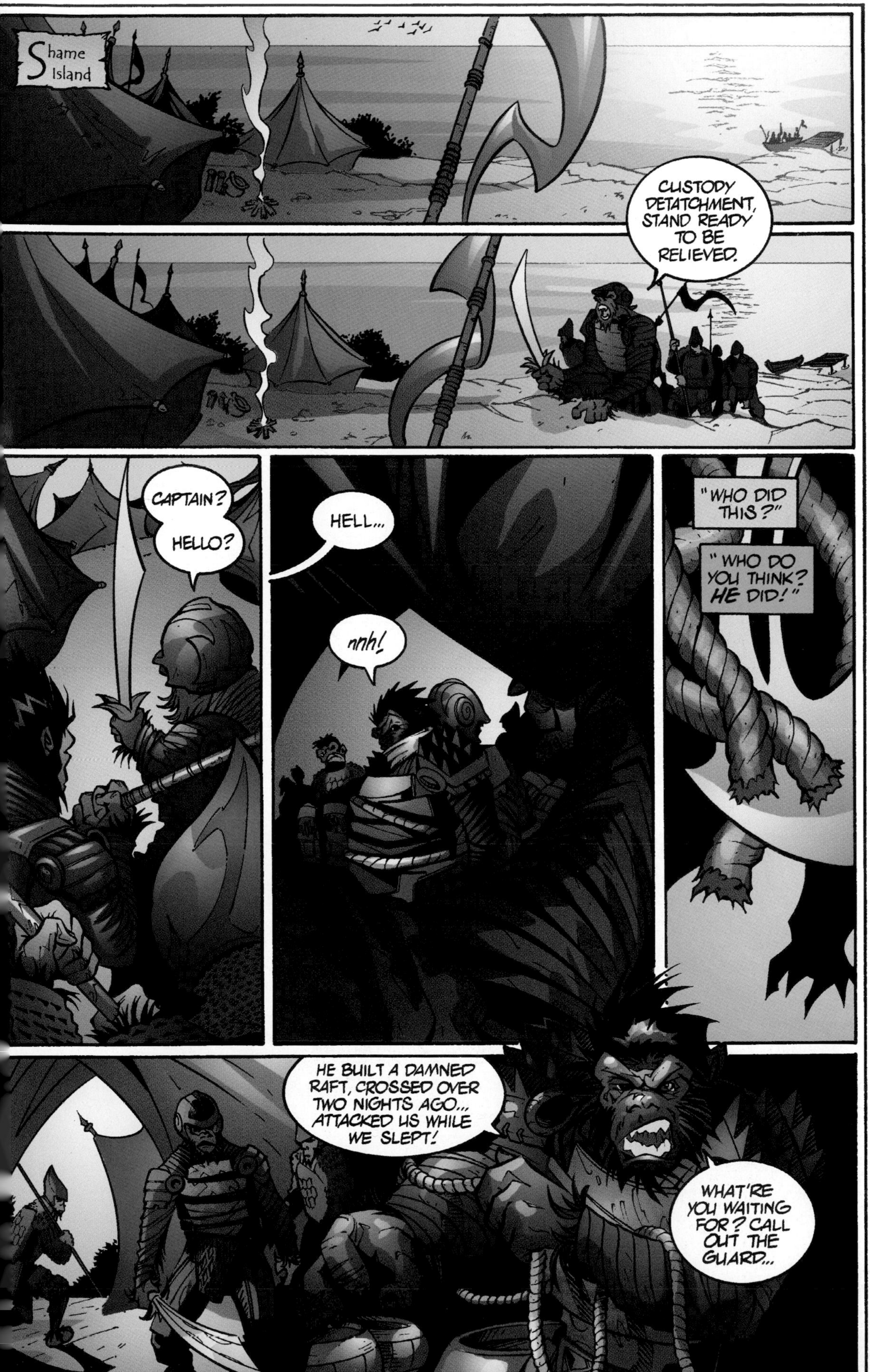
Shame Island
CUSTODY DETATCHMENT, STAND READY TO BE RELIEVED.
CAPTAIN?
HELLO?
HELL...
nnh!
"WHO DID THIS?"
"WHO DO YOU THINK? HE DID!"
HE BUILT A DAMNED RAFT, CROSSED OVER TWO NIGHTS AGO... ATTACKED US WHILE WE SLEPT!
WHAT'RE YOU WAITING FOR? CALL OUT THE GUARD...

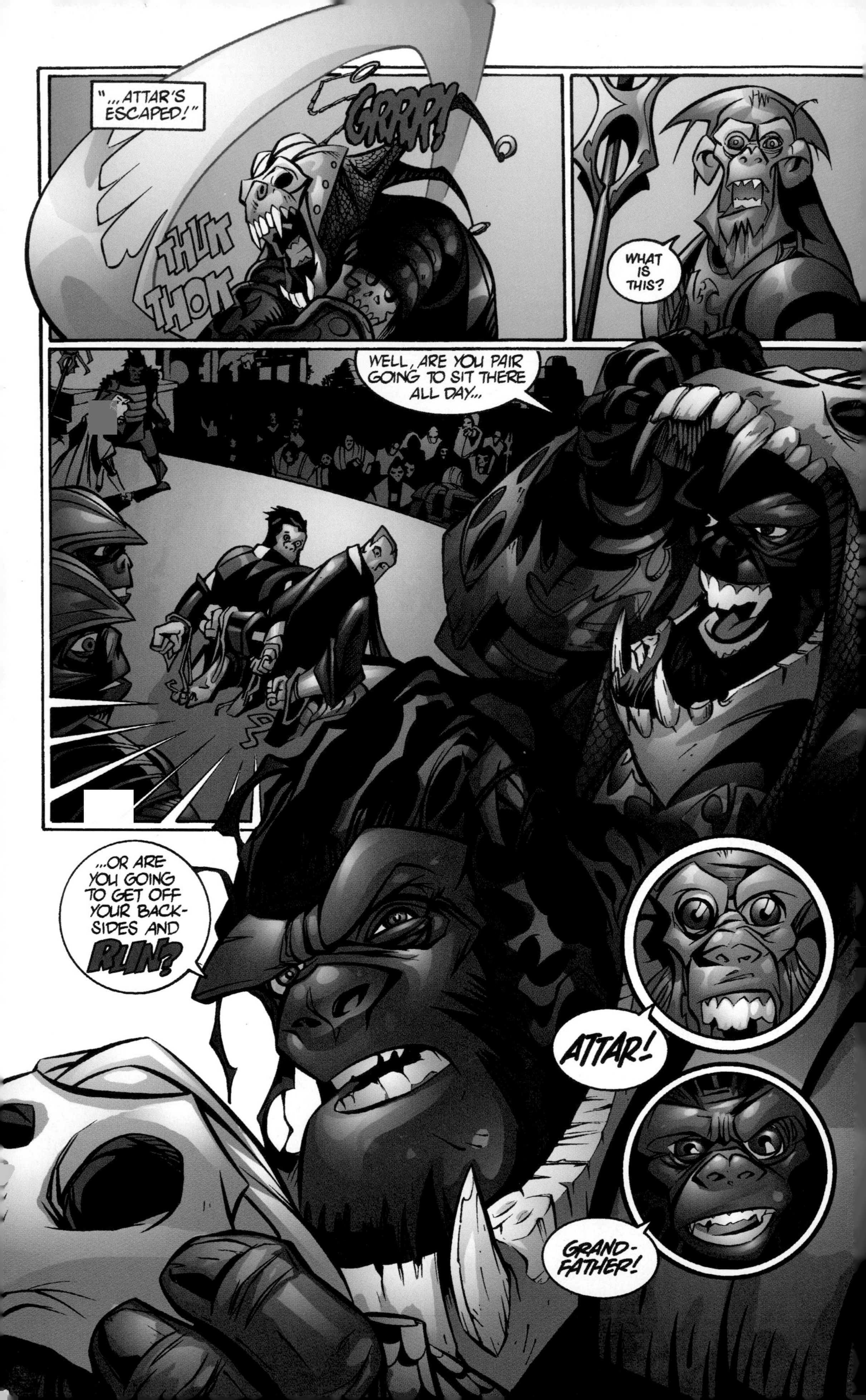
"...ATTAR'S ESCAPED!"
GRRRP!
THUK THOK
WHAT IS THIS?
WELL, ARE YOU PAIR GOING TO SIT THERE ALL DAY...
...OR ARE YOU GOING TO GET OFF YOUR BACK-SIDES AND RUN?
ATTAR!
GRAND-FATHER!

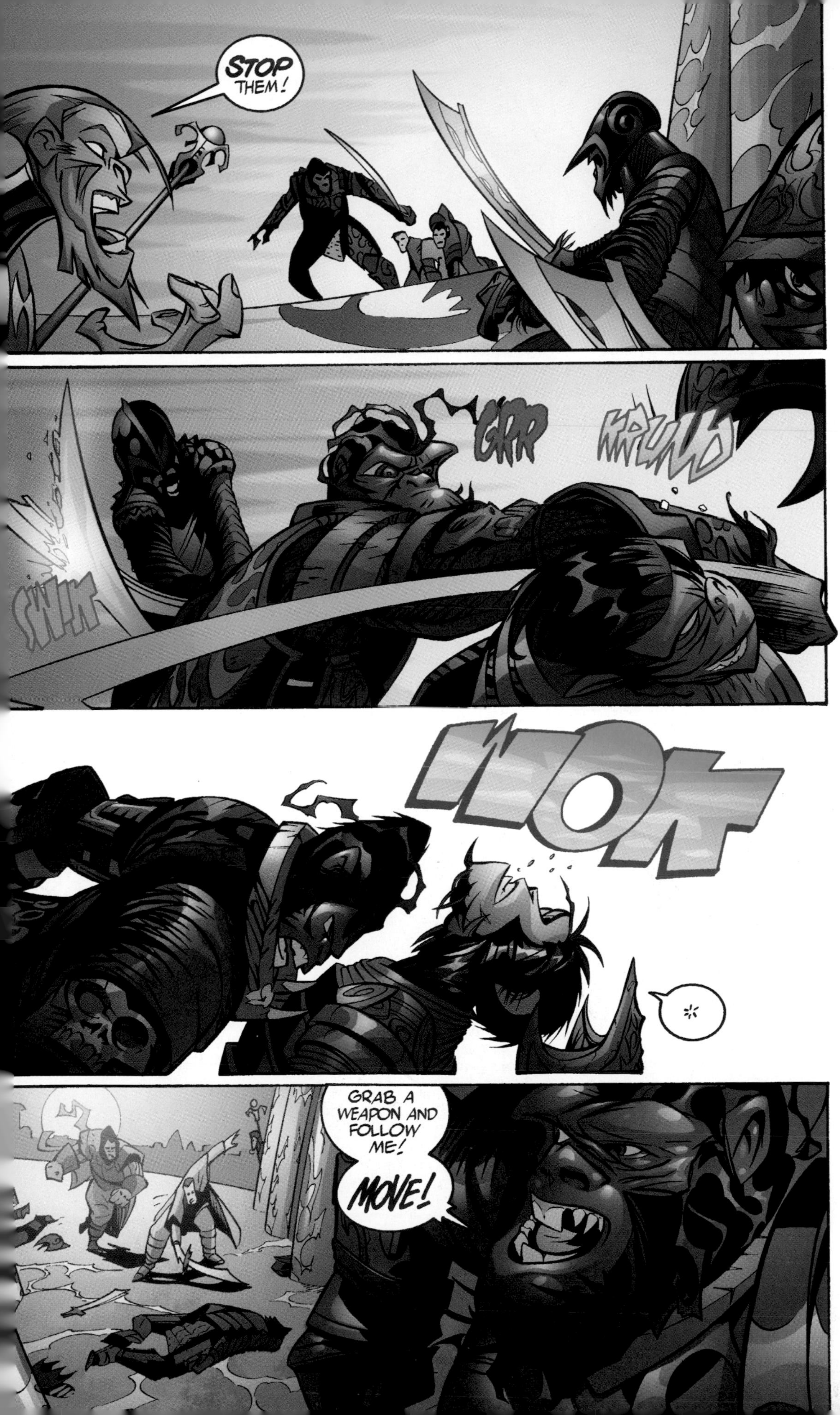
STOP THEM!
GRR
KRUNG
GRAB A WEAPON AND FOLLOW ME!
MOVE!

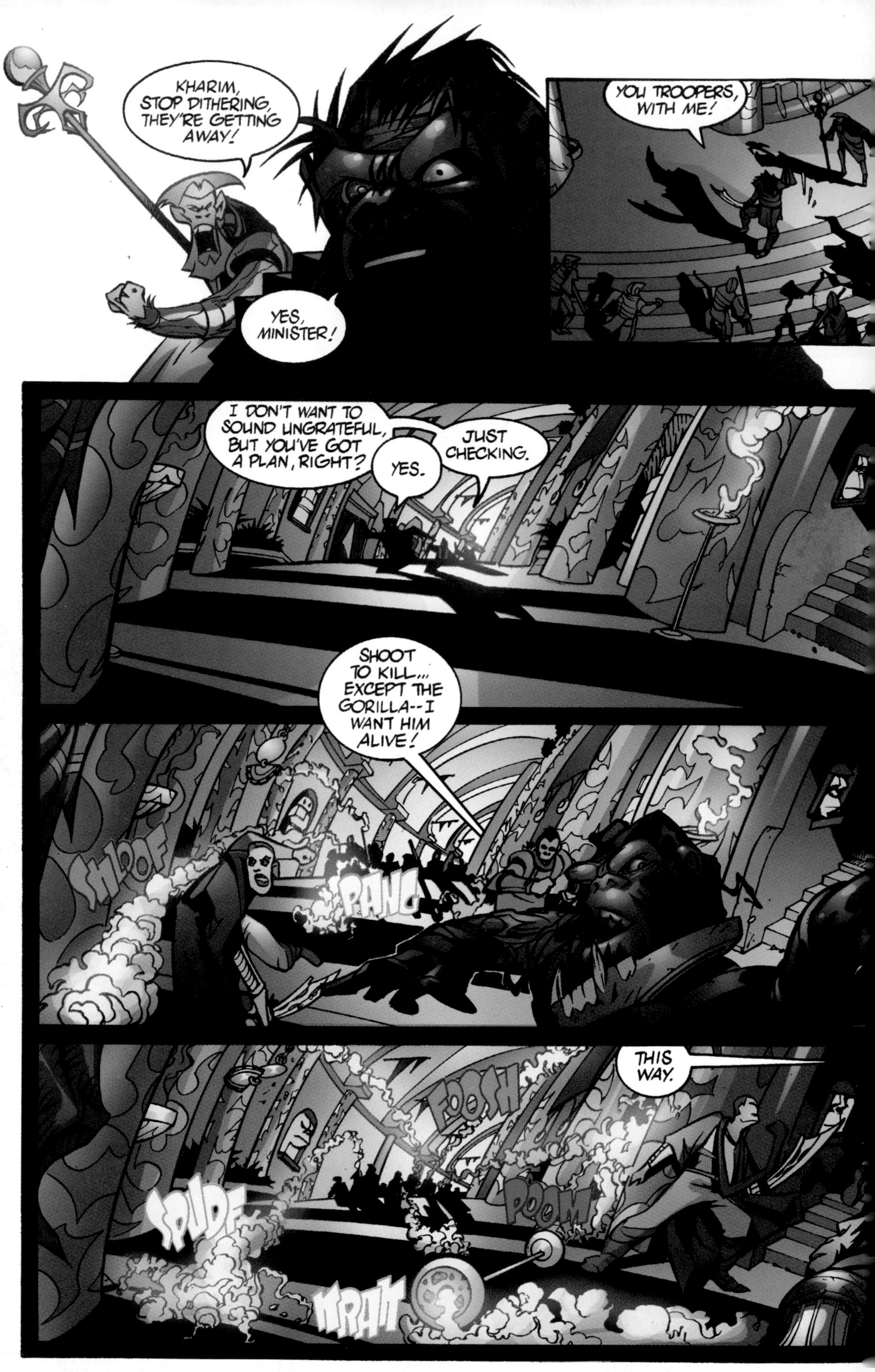
KHARIM, STOP DITHERING, THEY'RE GETTING AWAY!
YES, MINISTER!
YOU TROOPERS, WITH ME!
I DON'T WANT TO SOUND UNGRATEFUL, BUT YOU'VE GOT A PLAN, RIGHT?
YES.
JUST CHECKING.
SHOOT TO KILL... EXCEPT THE GORILLA--I WANT HIM ALIVE!
SHOOF
PANG
THIS WAY.
FOOSH
POOM
SPUDF
MRAH

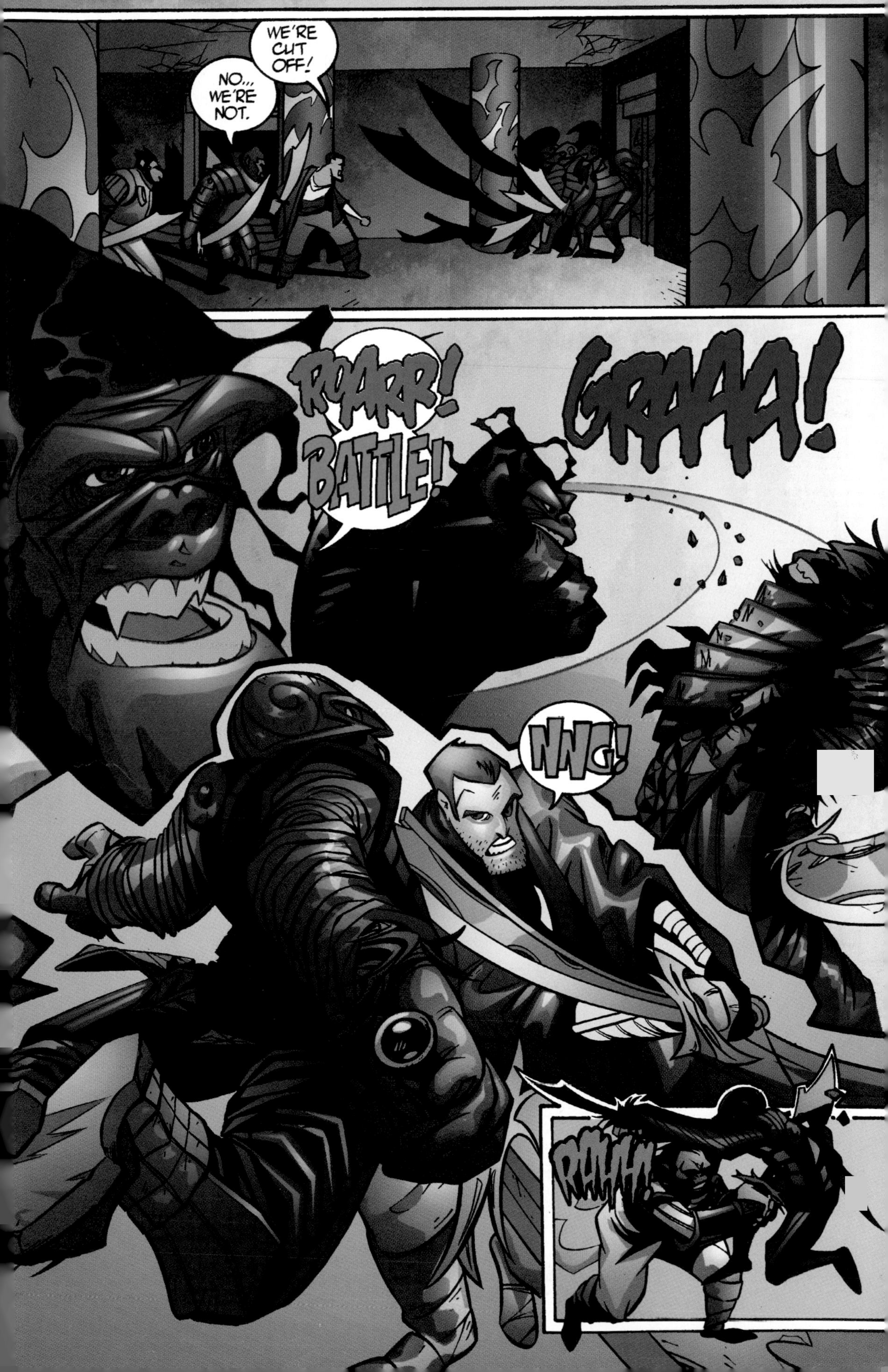
WE'RE CUT OFF!
NO... WE'RE NOT.
ROARR! BATTLE!
GRAAAA!
NNG!
RAAAH!

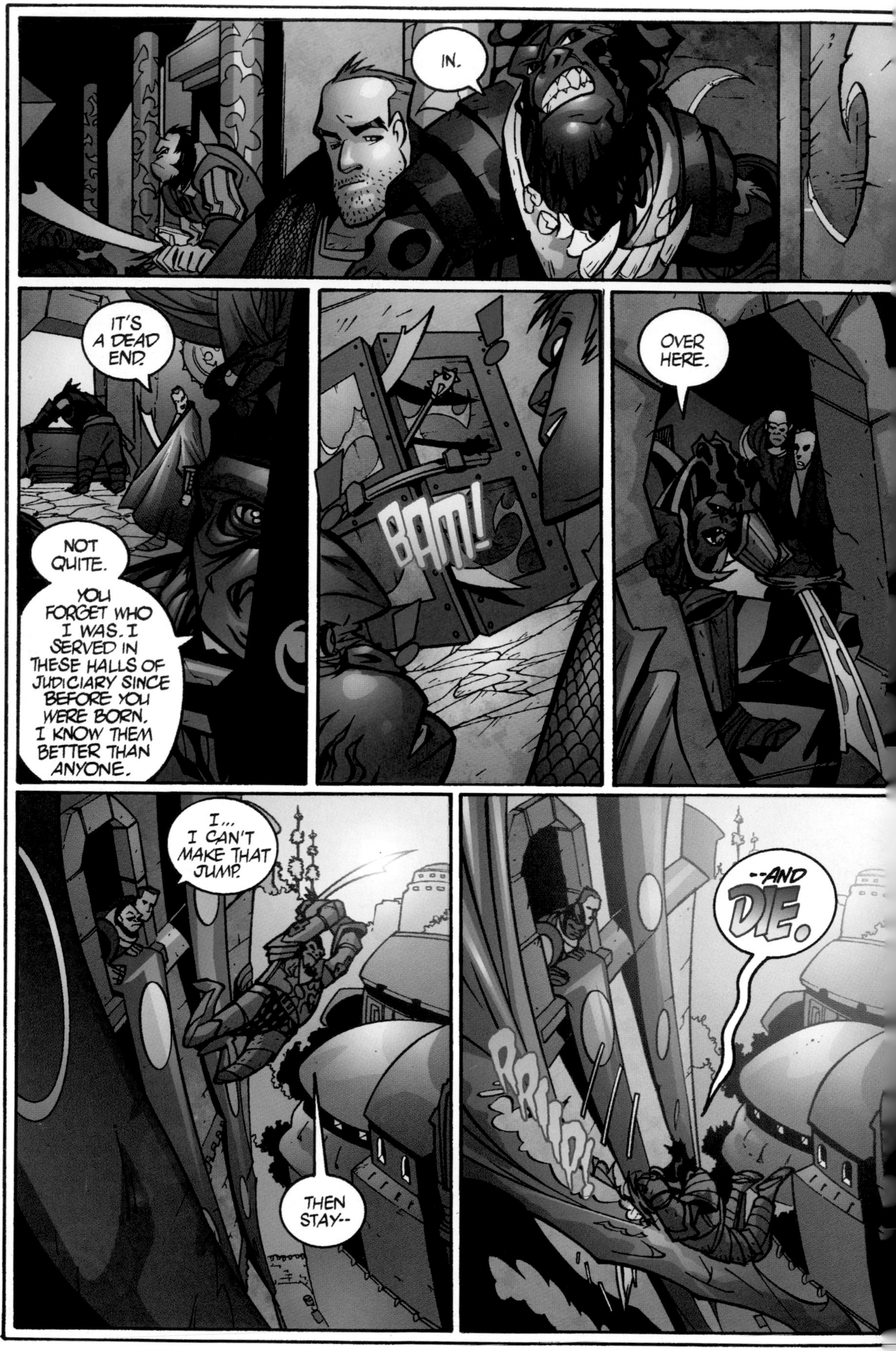
IN.
IT'S A DEAD END.
NOT QUITE.
YOU FORGET WHO I WAS. I SERVED IN THESE HALLS OF JUDICIARY SINCE BEFORE YOU WERE BORN. I KNOW THEM BETTER THAN ANYONE.
BAM!
OVER HERE.
I... I CAN'T MAKE THAT JUMP.
THEN STAY--
--AND DIE.

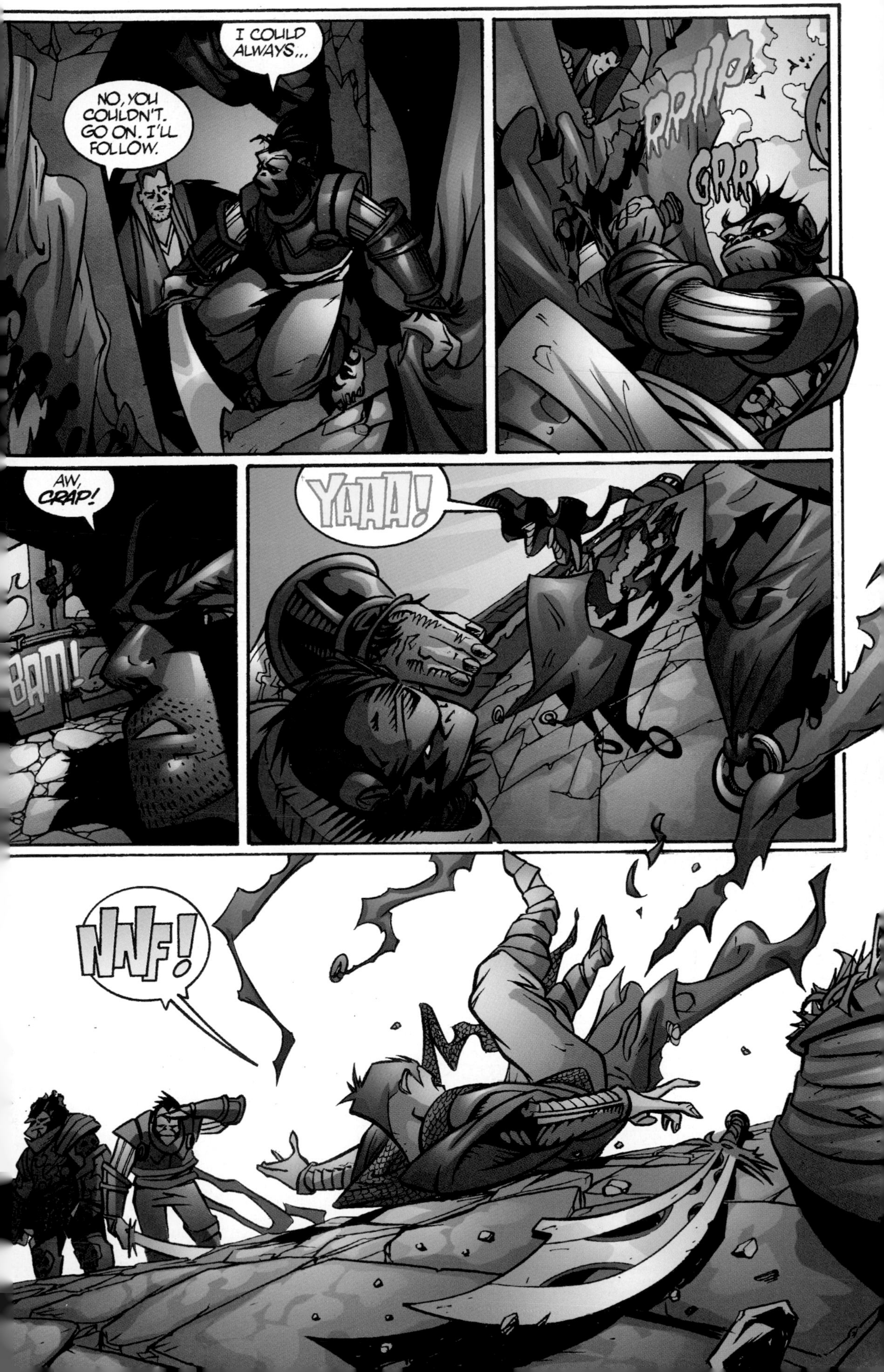
I COULD ALWAYS...
NO, YOU COULDN'T. GO ON. I'LL FOLLOW.
RRIIP
GRR
AW, CRAP!
BAM!
YAAA!
NNF!

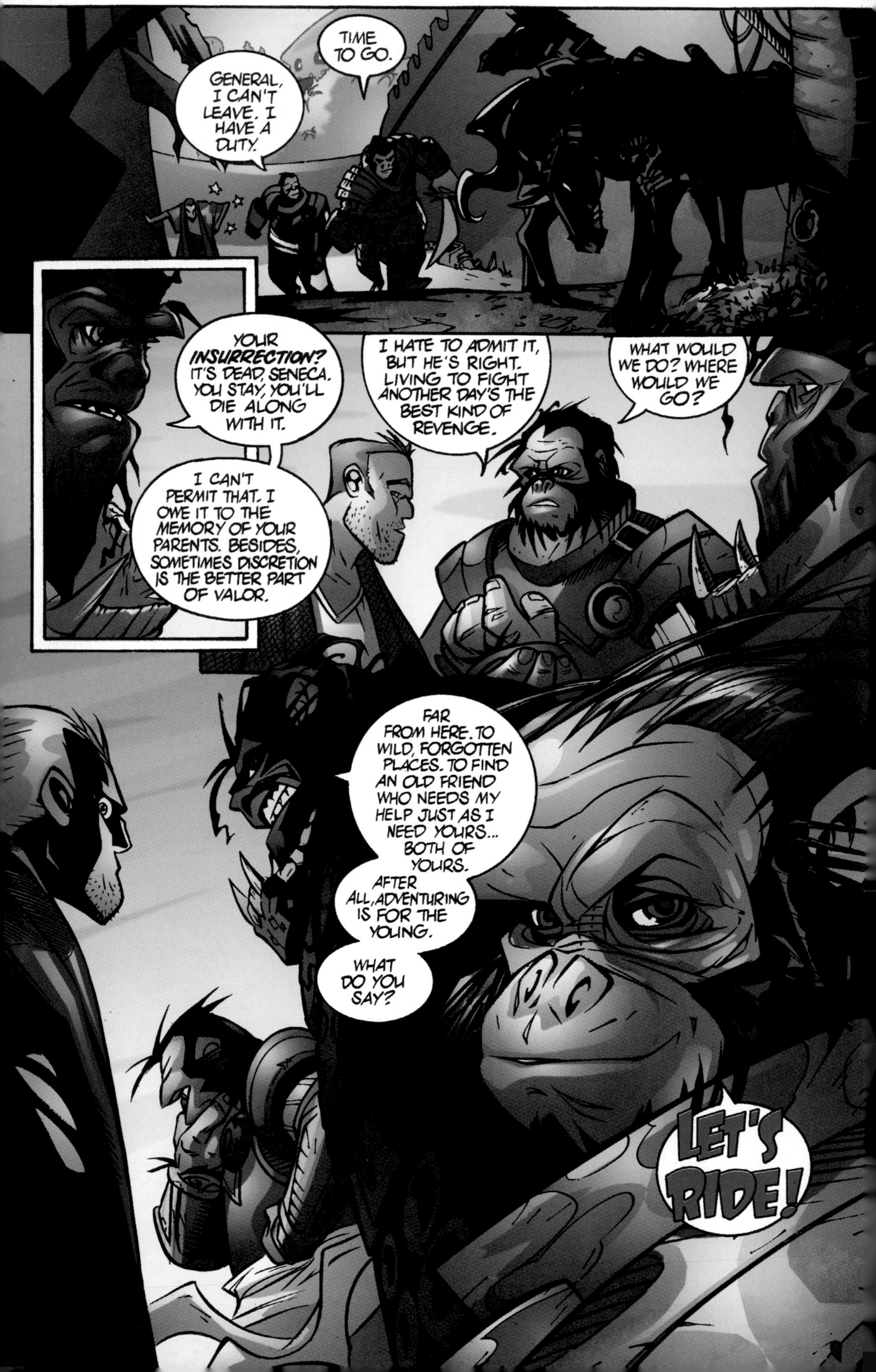
GENERAL, I CAN'T LEAVE. I HAVE A DUTY.
TIME TO GO.
YOUR *INSURRECTION?* IT'S DEAD, SENECA. YOU STAY, YOU'LL DIE ALONG WITH IT.
I CAN'T PERMIT THAT. I OWE IT TO THE MEMORY OF YOUR PARENTS. BESIDES, SOMETIMES DISCRETION IS THE BETTER PART OF VALOR.
I HATE TO ADMIT IT, BUT HE'S RIGHT. LIVING TO FIGHT ANOTHER DAY'S THE BEST KIND OF REVENGE.
WHAT WOULD WE DO? WHERE WOULD WE GO?
FAR FROM HERE. TO WILD, FORGOTTEN PLACES. TO FIND AN OLD FRIEND WHO NEEDS MY HELP JUST AS I NEED YOURS... BOTH OF YOURS.
AFTER ALL, ADVENTURING IS FOR THE YOUNG.
WHAT DO YOU SAY?
LET'S RIDE!

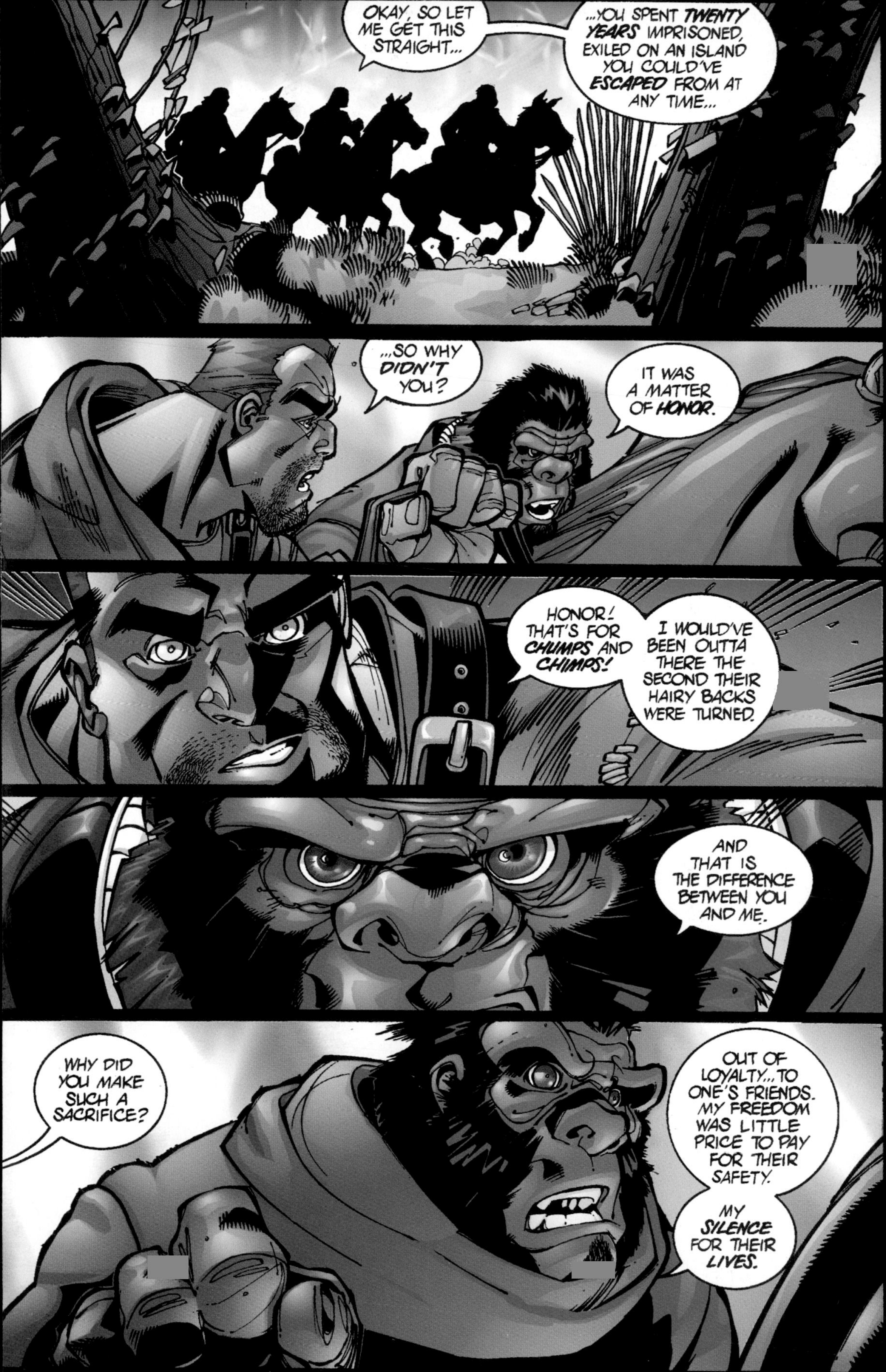
OKAY, SO LET ME GET THIS STRAIGHT...
...YOU SPENT TWENTY YEARS IMPRISONED, EXILED ON AN ISLAND YOU COULD'VE ESCAPED FROM AT ANY TIME...
...SO WHY DIDN'T YOU?
IT WAS A MATTER OF HONOR.
HONOR! THAT'S FOR CHUMPS AND CHIMPS!
I WOULD'VE BEEN OUTTA THERE THE SECOND THEIR HAIRY BACKS WERE TURNED.
AND THAT IS THE DIFFERENCE BETWEEN YOU AND ME.
WHY DID YOU MAKE SUCH A SACRIFICE?
OUT OF LOYALTY... TO ONE'S FRIENDS. MY FREEDOM WAS LITTLE PRICE TO PAY FOR THEIR SAFETY.
MY SILENCE FOR THEIR LIVES.

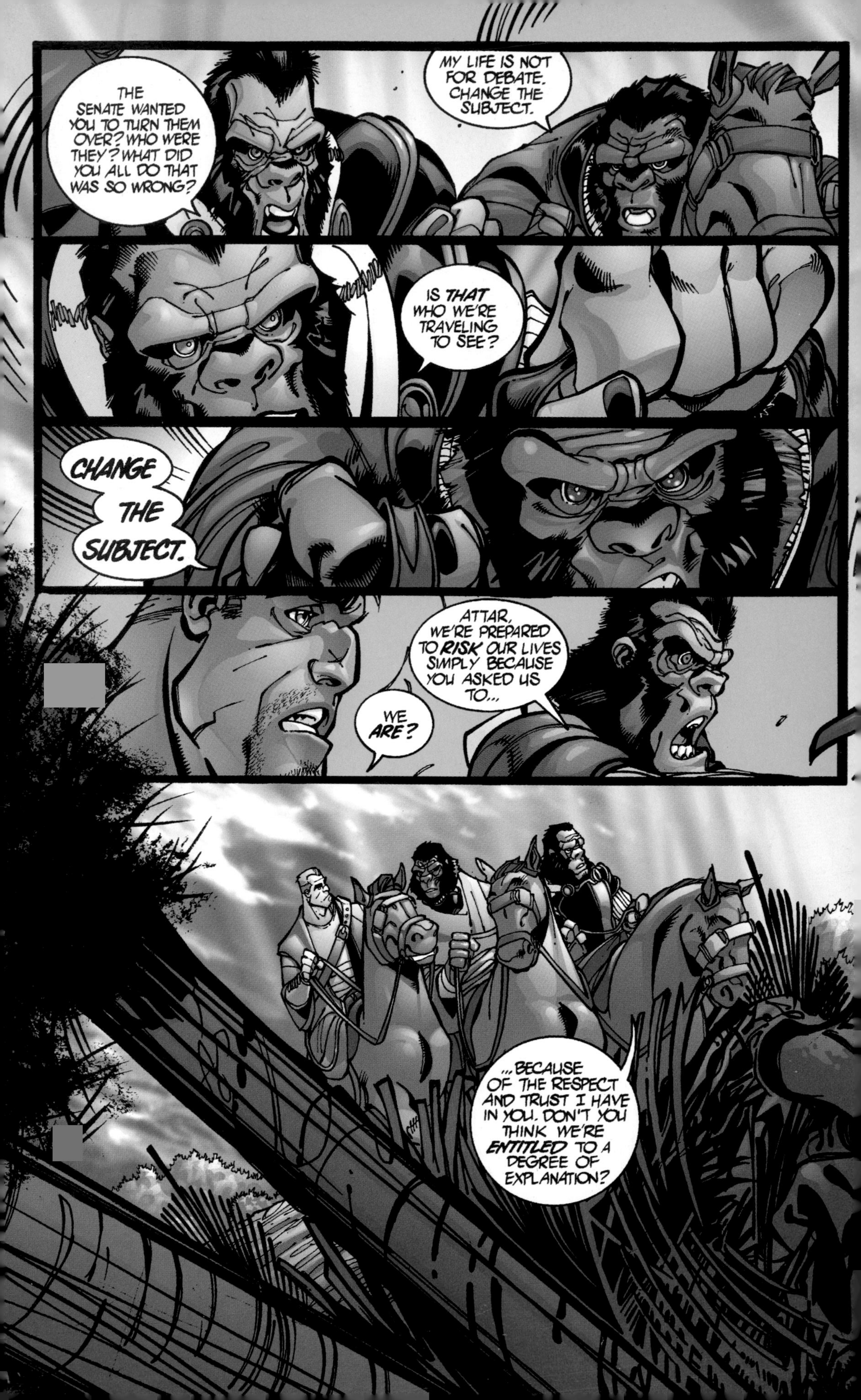
THE SENATE WANTED YOU TO TURN THEM OVER? WHO WERE THEY? WHAT DID YOU ALL DO THAT WAS SO WRONG?
MY LIFE IS NOT FOR DEBATE. CHANGE THE SUBJECT.
IS THAT WHO WE'RE TRAVELING TO SEE?
CHANGE THE SUBJECT.
ATTAR, WE'RE PREPARED TO RISK OUR LIVES SIMPLY BECAUSE YOU ASKED US TO...
WE ARE?
...BECAUSE OF THE RESPECT AND TRUST I HAVE IN YOU. DON'T YOU THINK WE'RE ENTITLED TO A DEGREE OF EXPLANATION?

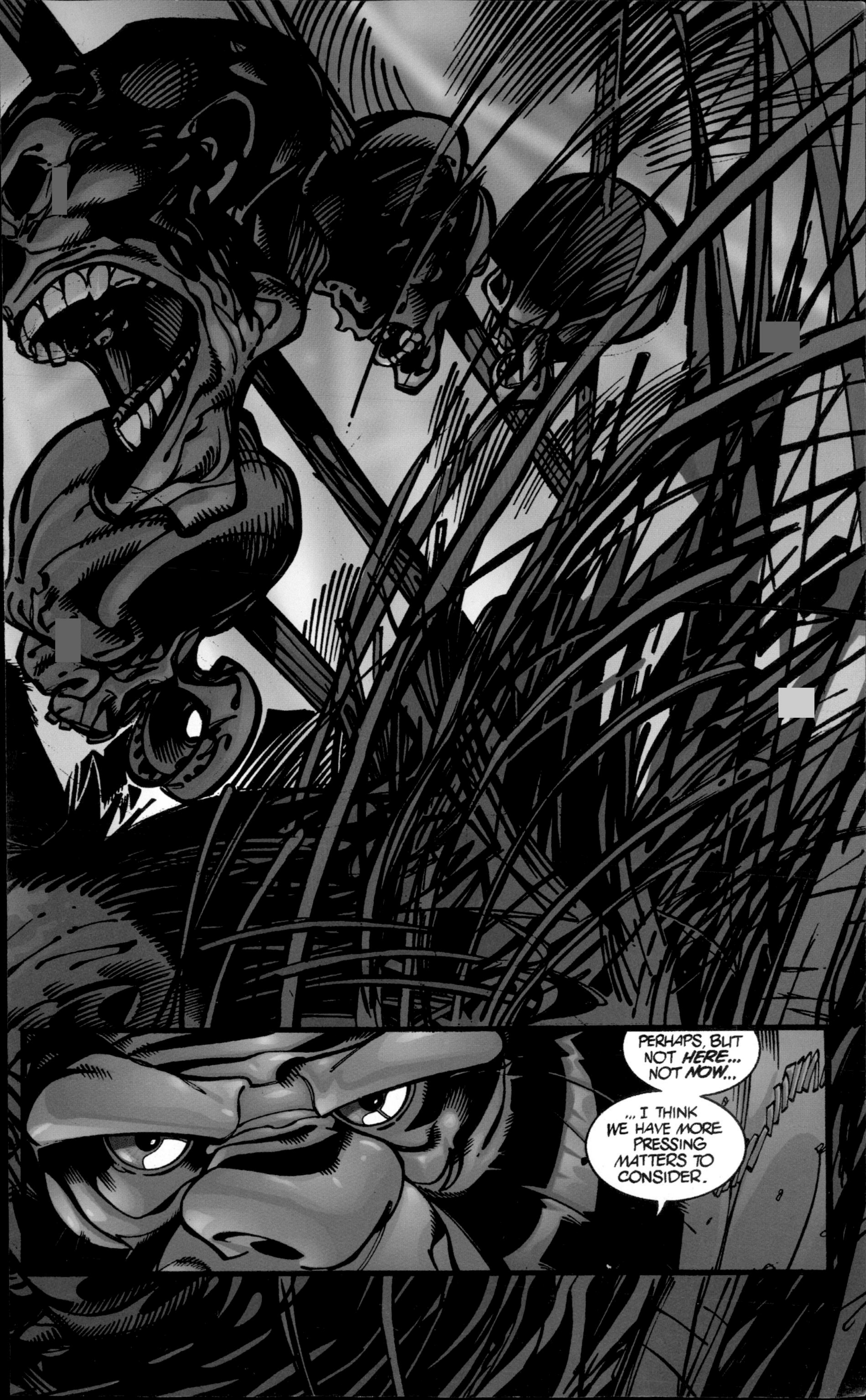
PERHAPS, BUT NOT *HERE*... NOT *NOW*...
... I THINK WE HAVE MORE PRESSING MATTERS TO CONSIDER.

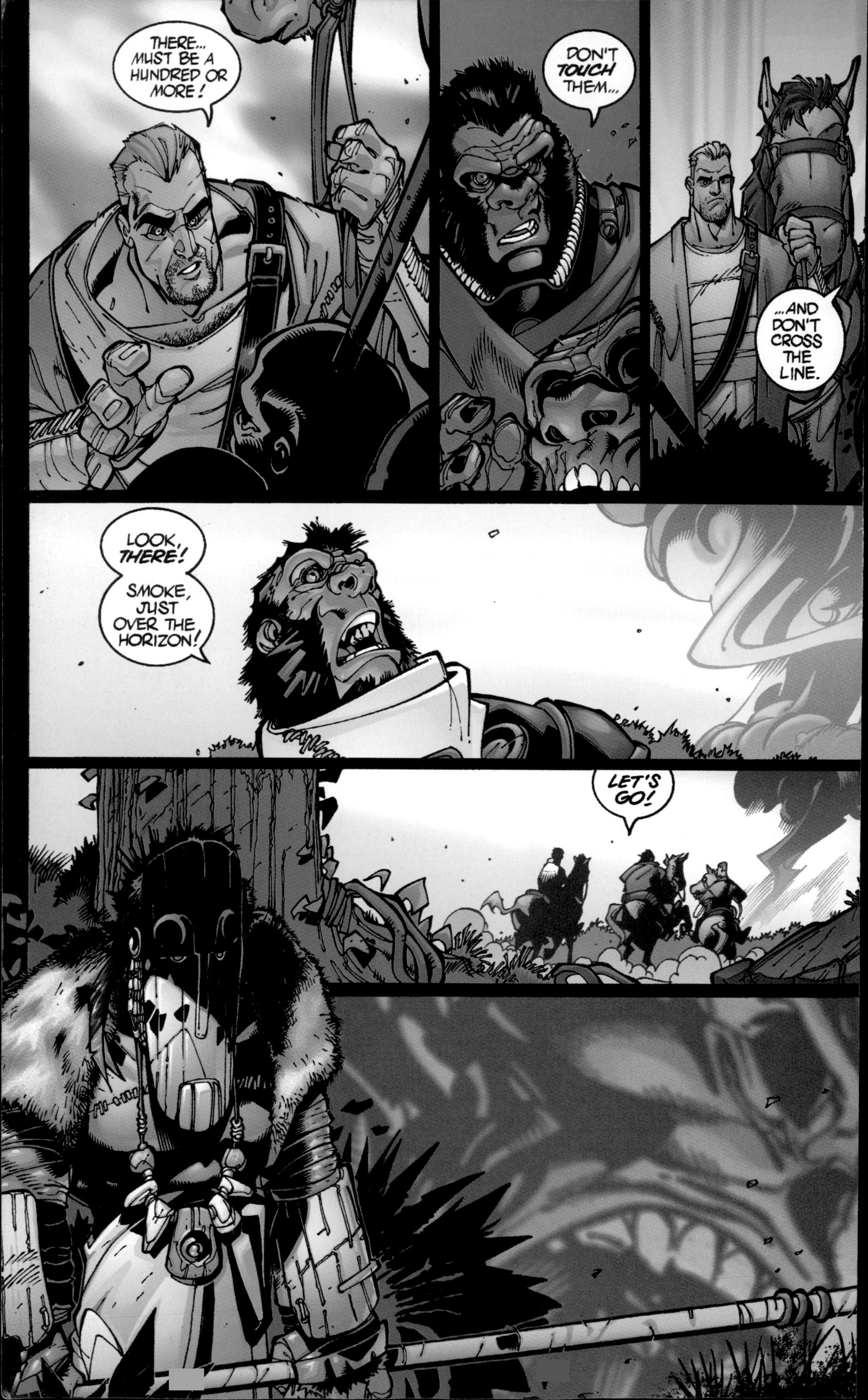
THERE... MUST BE A HUNDRED OR MORE!
DON'T TOUCH THEM...
...AND DON'T CROSS THE LINE.
LOOK, THERE!
SMOKE, JUST OVER THE HORIZON!
LET'S GO!

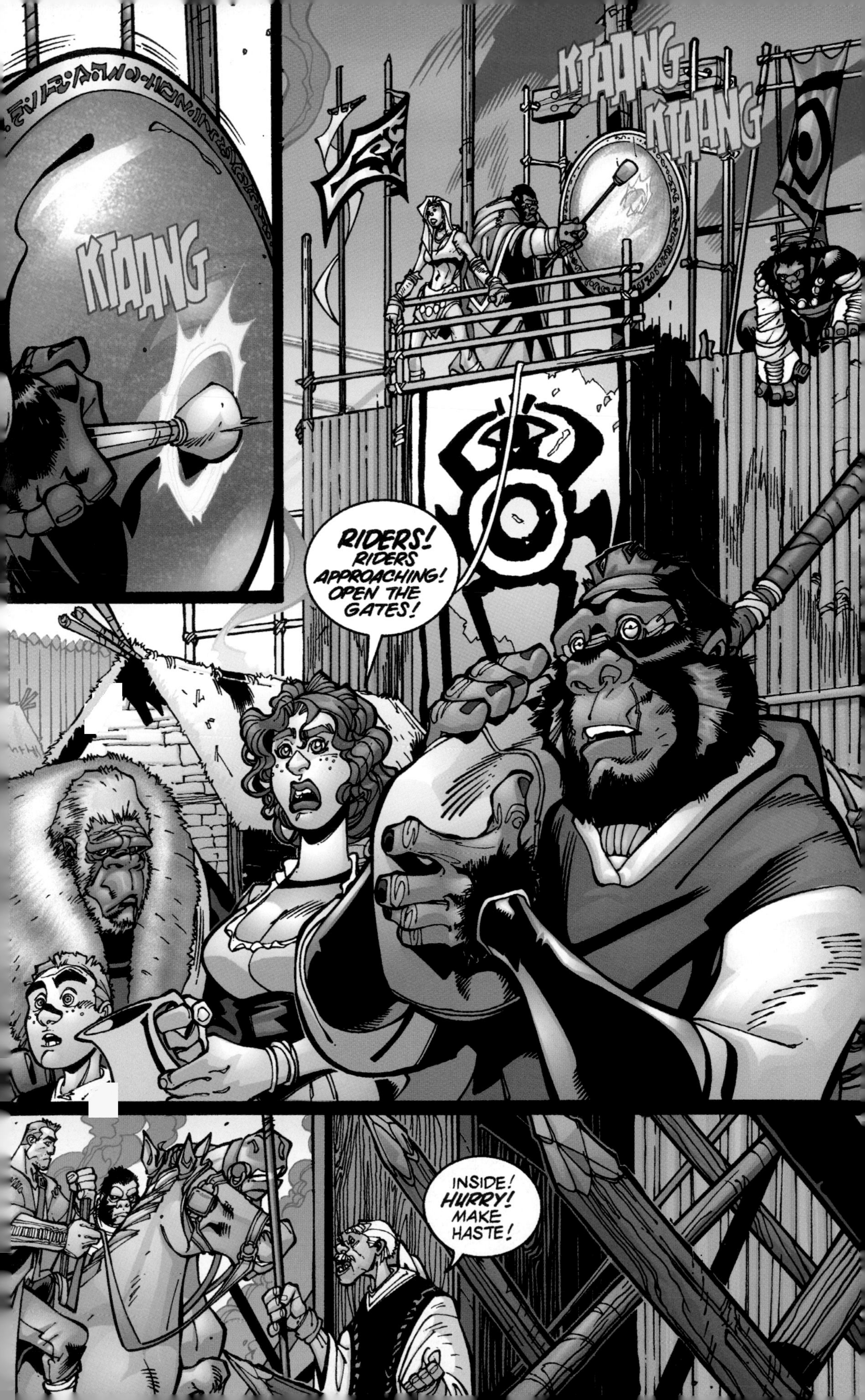
KTAANG
KTAANG
KTAANG
RIDERS! RIDERS APPROACHING! OPEN THE GATES!
INSIDE! HURRY! MAKE HASTE!

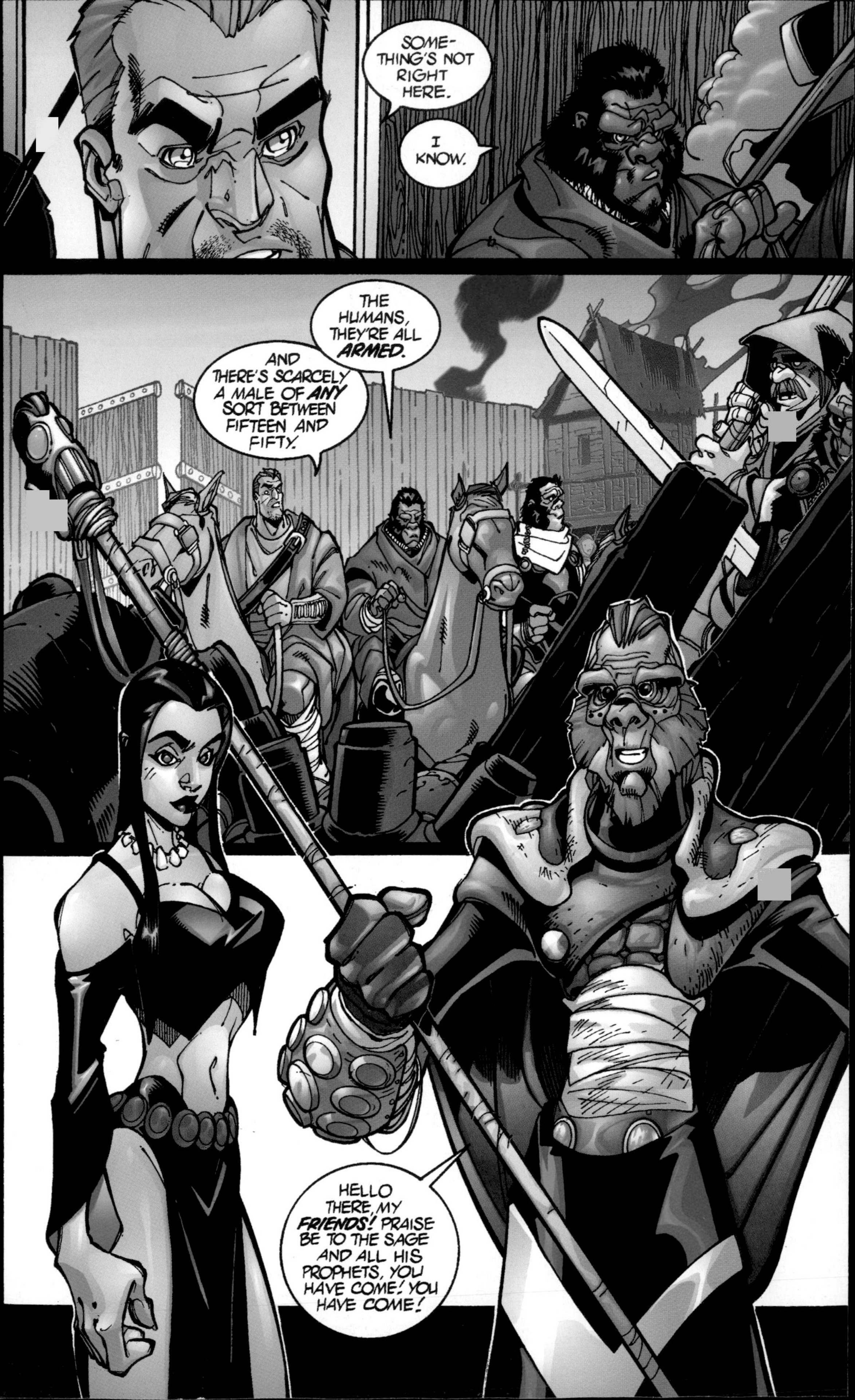
SOMETHING'S NOT RIGHT HERE.
I KNOW.
THE HUMANS, THEY'RE ALL ARMED.
AND THERE'S SCARCELY A MALE OF ANY SORT BETWEEN FIFTEEN AND FIFTY.
HELLO THERE, MY FRIENDS! PRAISE BE TO THE SAGE AND ALL HIS PROPHETS, YOU HAVE COME! YOU HAVE COME!

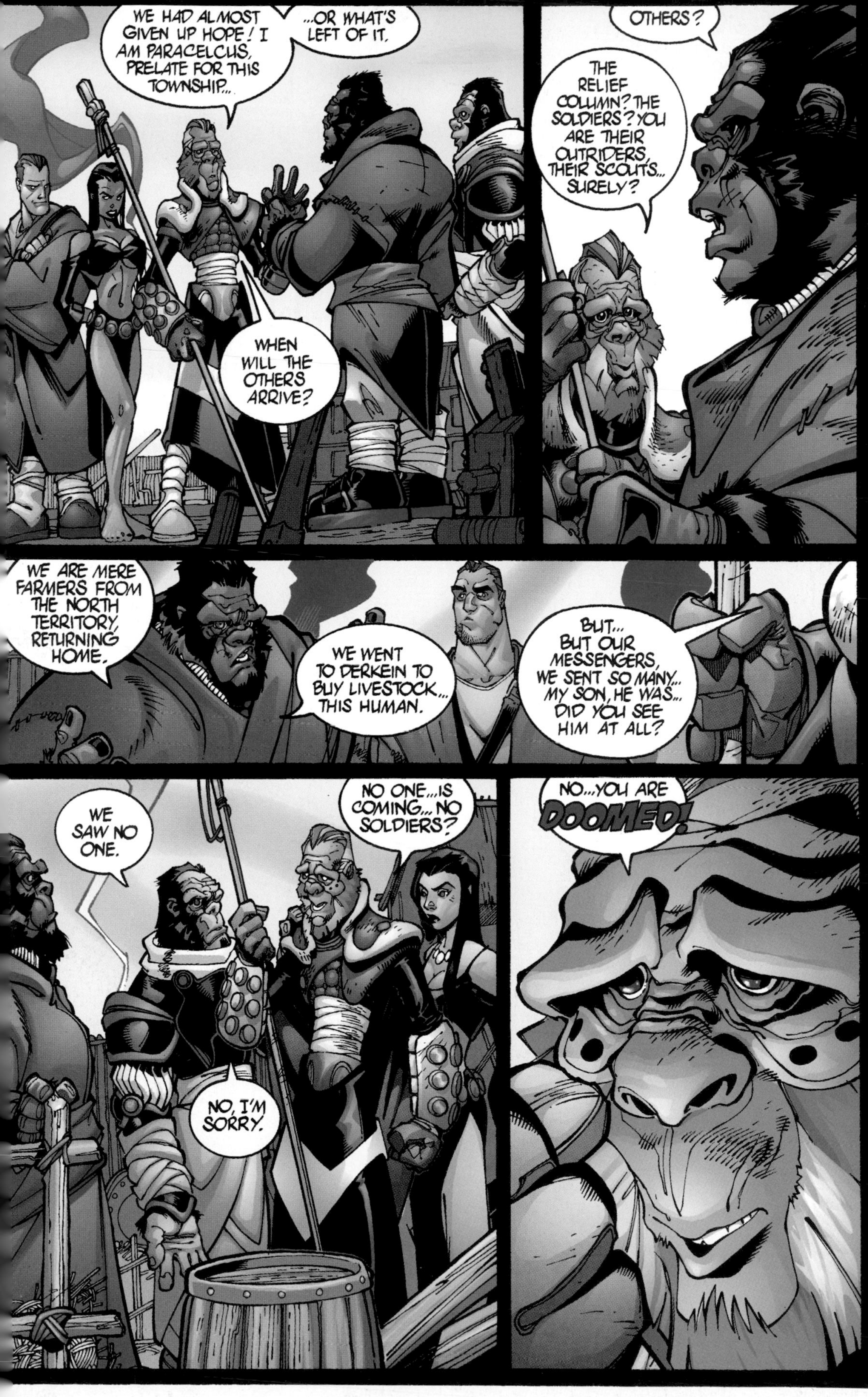
WE HAD ALMOST GIVEN UP HOPE! I AM PARACELCUS, PRELATE FOR THIS TOWNSHIP...
...OR WHAT'S LEFT OF IT.
WHEN WILL THE OTHERS ARRIVE?
OTHERS?
THE RELIEF COLUMN? THE SOLDIERS? YOU ARE THEIR OUTRIDERS, THEIR SCOUTS... SURELY?
WE ARE MERE FARMERS FROM THE NORTH TERRITORY, RETURNING HOME.
WE WENT TO DERKEIN TO BUY LIVESTOCK... THIS HUMAN.
BUT... BUT OUR MESSENGERS, WE SENT SO MANY... MY SON, HE WAS... DID YOU SEE HIM AT ALL?
WE SAW NO ONE.
NO, I'M SORRY.
NO ONE... IS COMING... NO SOLDIERS?
NO... YOU ARE DOOMED!

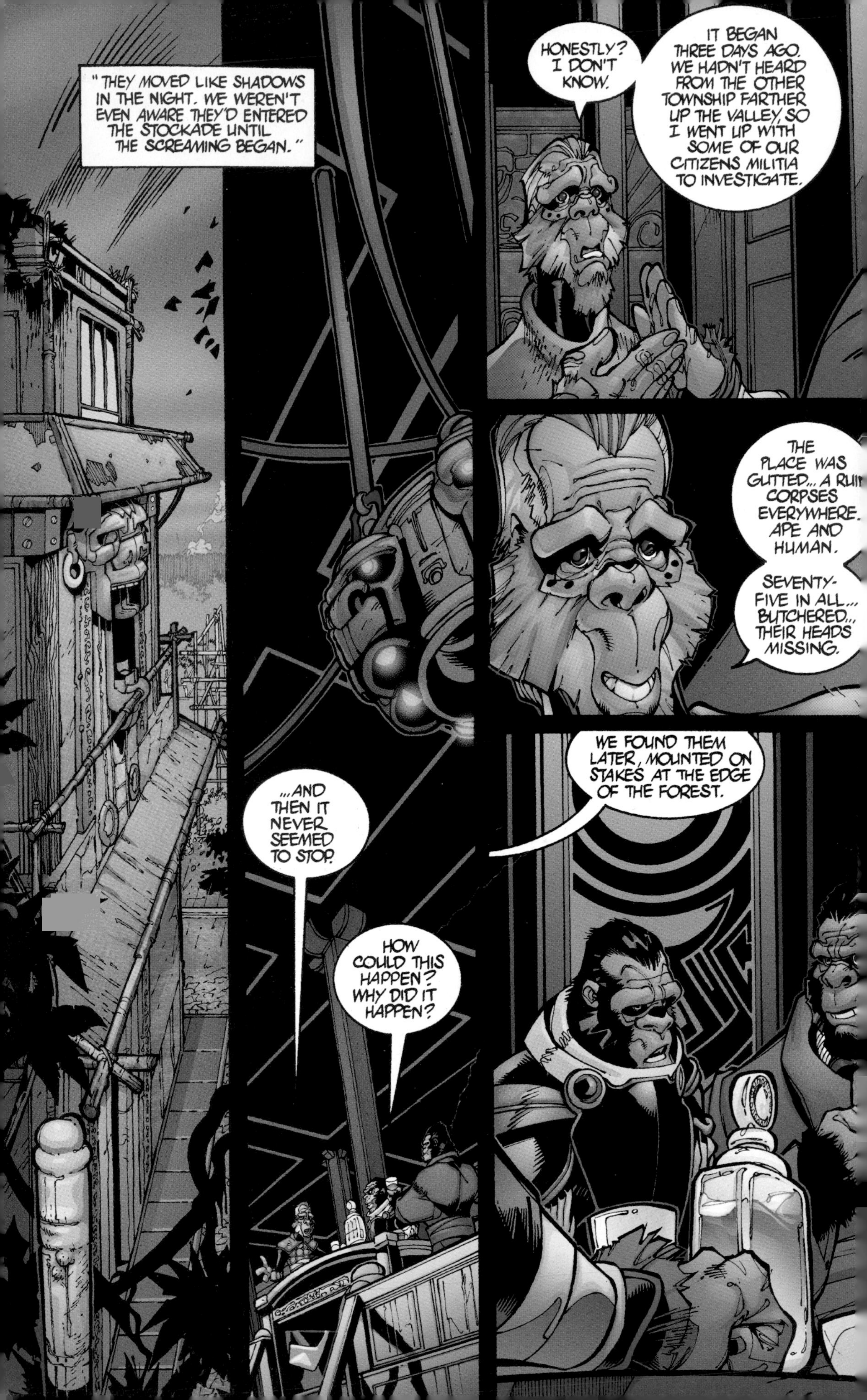
"THEY MOVED LIKE SHADOWS IN THE NIGHT. WE WEREN'T EVEN AWARE THEY'D ENTERED THE STOCKADE UNTIL THE SCREAMING BEGAN."
...AND THEN IT NEVER SEEMED TO STOP.
HOW COULD THIS HAPPEN? WHY DID IT HAPPEN?
HONESTLY? I DON'T KNOW.
IT BEGAN THREE DAYS AGO. WE HADN'T HEARD FROM THE OTHER TOWNSHIP FARTHER UP THE VALLEY, SO I WENT UP WITH SOME OF OUR CITIZENS MILITIA TO INVESTIGATE.
THE PLACE WAS GUTTED... A RUI
CORPSES EVERYWHERE. APE AND HUMAN.
SEVENTY-FIVE IN ALL... BUTCHERED... THEIR HEADS MISSING.
WE FOUND THEM LATER, MOUNTED ON STAKES AT THE EDGE OF THE FOREST.

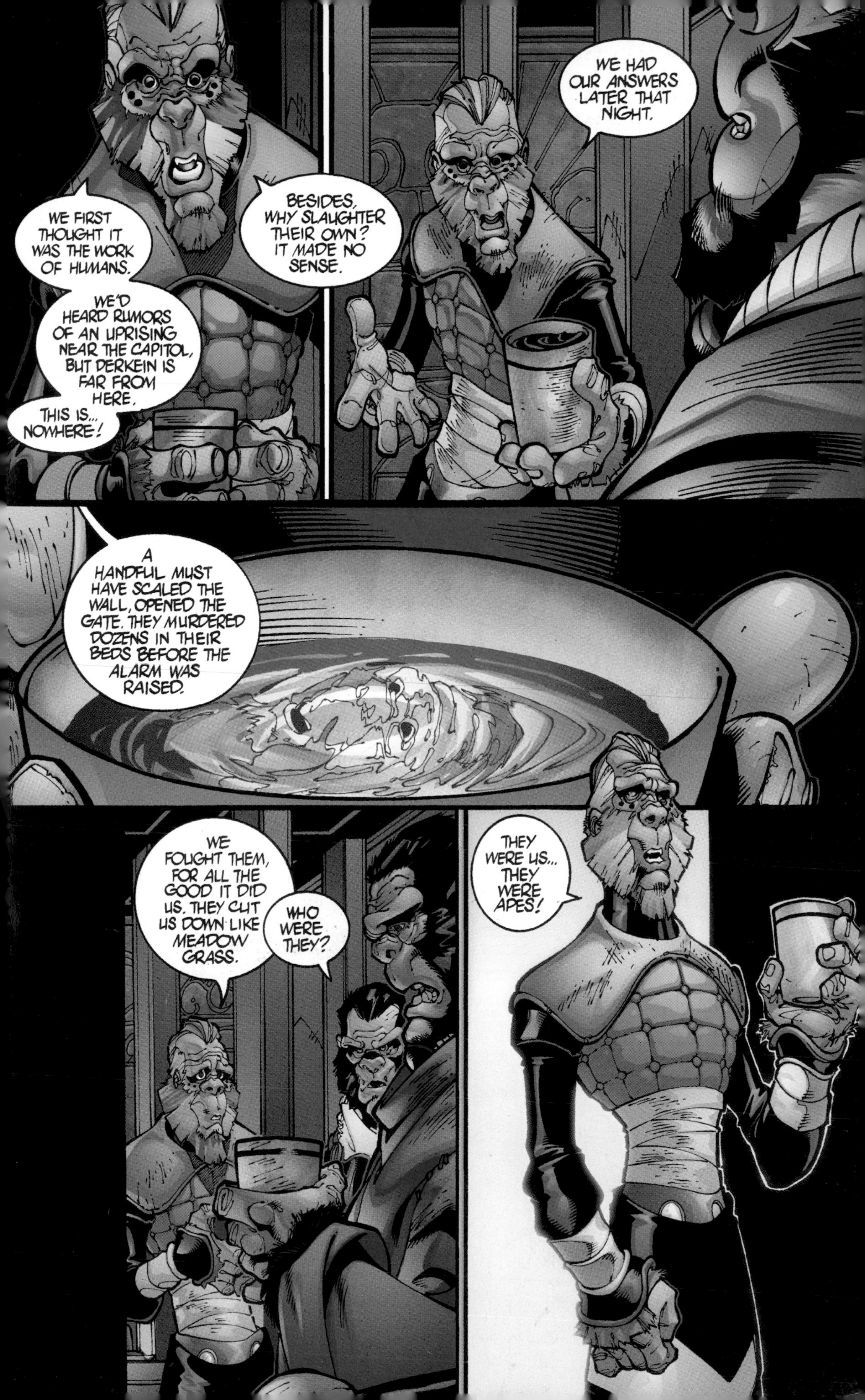
WE FIRST THOUGHT IT WAS THE WORK OF HUMANS.
WE'D HEARD RUMORS OF AN UPRISING NEAR THE CAPITOL, BUT DERKEIN IS FAR FROM HERE.
THIS IS... NOWHERE!
BESIDES, WHY SLAUGHTER THEIR OWN? IT MADE NO SENSE.
WE HAD OUR ANSWERS LATER THAT NIGHT.
A HANDFUL MUST HAVE SCALED THE WALL, OPENED THE GATE. THEY MURDERED DOZENS IN THEIR BEDS BEFORE THE ALARM WAS RAISED.
WE FOUGHT THEM, FOR ALL THE GOOD IT DID US. THEY CUT US DOWN LIKE MEADOW GRASS.
WHO WERE THEY?
THEY WERE US... THEY WERE APES!

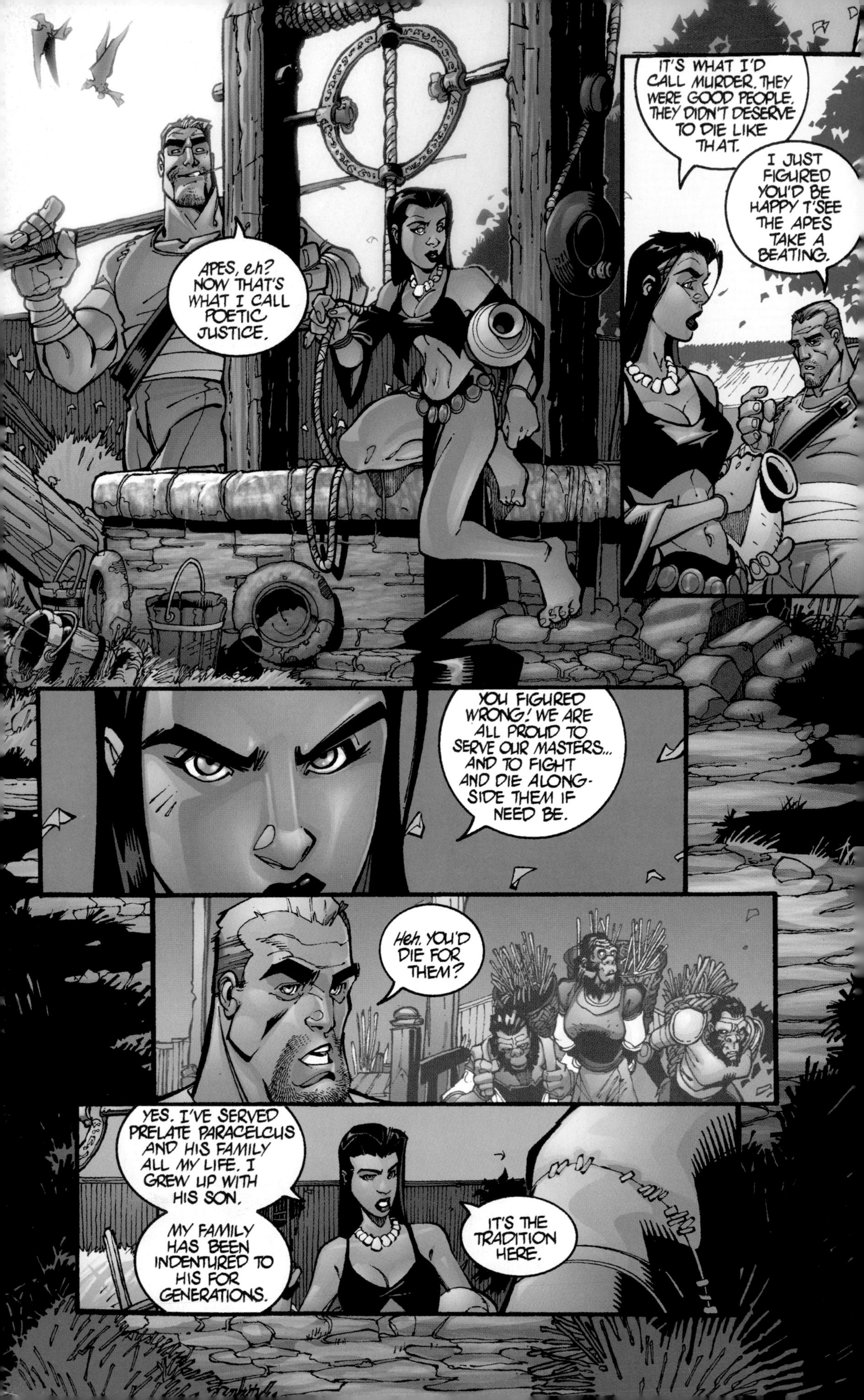
APES, eh? NOW THAT'S WHAT I CALL POETIC JUSTICE.
IT'S WHAT I'D CALL MURDER. THEY WERE GOOD PEOPLE. THEY DIDN'T DESERVE TO DIE LIKE THAT.
I JUST FIGURED YOU'D BE HAPPY T'SEE THE APES TAKE A BEATING.
YOU FIGURED WRONG! WE ARE ALL PROUD TO SERVE OUR MASTERS... AND TO FIGHT AND DIE ALONG-SIDE THEM IF NEED BE.
Heh. YOU'D DIE FOR THEM?
YES. I'VE SERVED PRELATE PARACELCUS AND HIS FAMILY ALL MY LIFE. I GREW UP WITH HIS SON.
MY FAMILY HAS BEEN INDENTURED TO HIS FOR GENERATIONS.
IT'S THE TRADITION HERE.

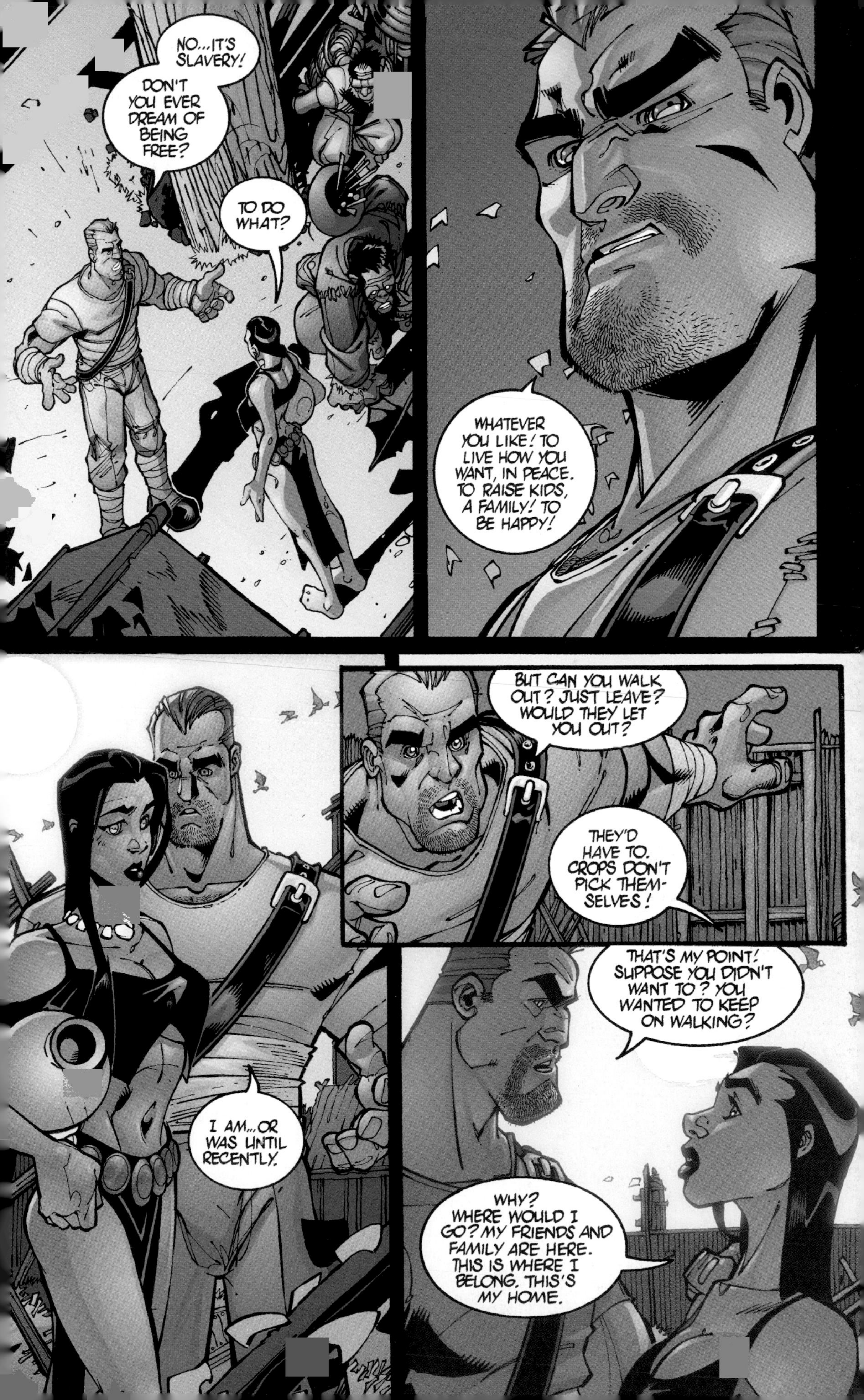
NO...IT'S SLAVERY!
DON'T YOU EVER DREAM OF BEING FREE?
TO DO WHAT?
WHATEVER YOU LIKE! TO LIVE HOW YOU WANT, IN PEACE. TO RAISE KIDS, A FAMILY! TO BE HAPPY!
I AM...OR WAS UNTIL RECENTLY.
BUT CAN YOU WALK OUT? JUST LEAVE? WOULD THEY LET YOU OUT?
THEY'D HAVE TO. CROPS DON'T PICK THEM-SELVES!
THAT'S MY POINT! SUPPOSE YOU DIDN'T WANT TO? YOU WANTED TO KEEP ON WALKING?
WHY? WHERE WOULD I GO? MY FRIENDS AND FAMILY ARE HERE. THIS IS WHERE I BELONG. THIS'S MY HOME.

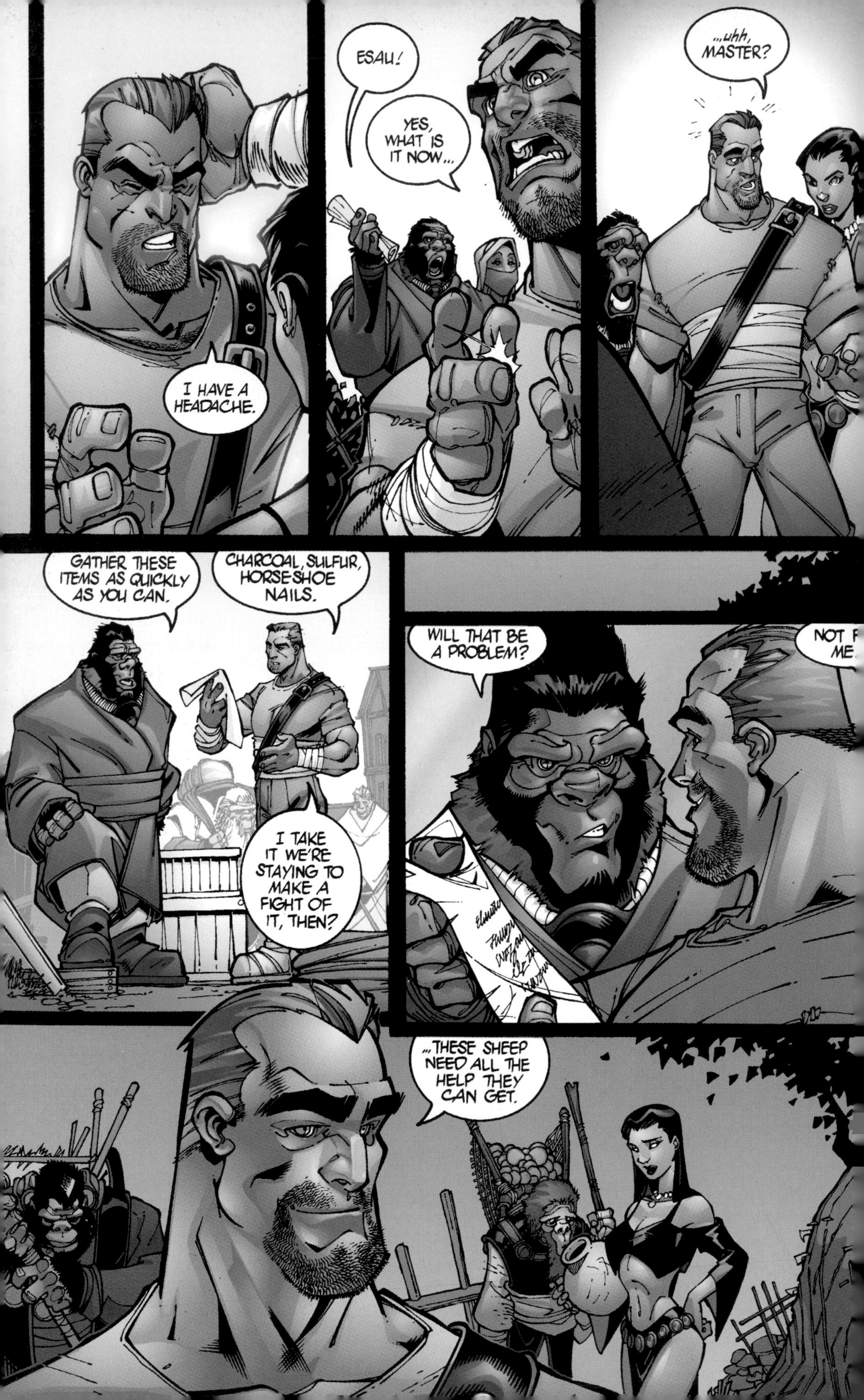
I HAVE A HEADACHE.
ESAU!
YES, WHAT IS IT NOW...
...uhh, MASTER?
GATHER THESE ITEMS AS QUICKLY AS YOU CAN.
CHARCOAL, SULFUR, HORSE-SHOE NAILS.
I TAKE IT WE'RE STAYING TO MAKE A FIGHT OF IT, THEN?
WILL THAT BE A PROBLEM?
NOT
...THESE SHEEP NEED ALL THE HELP THEY CAN GET.

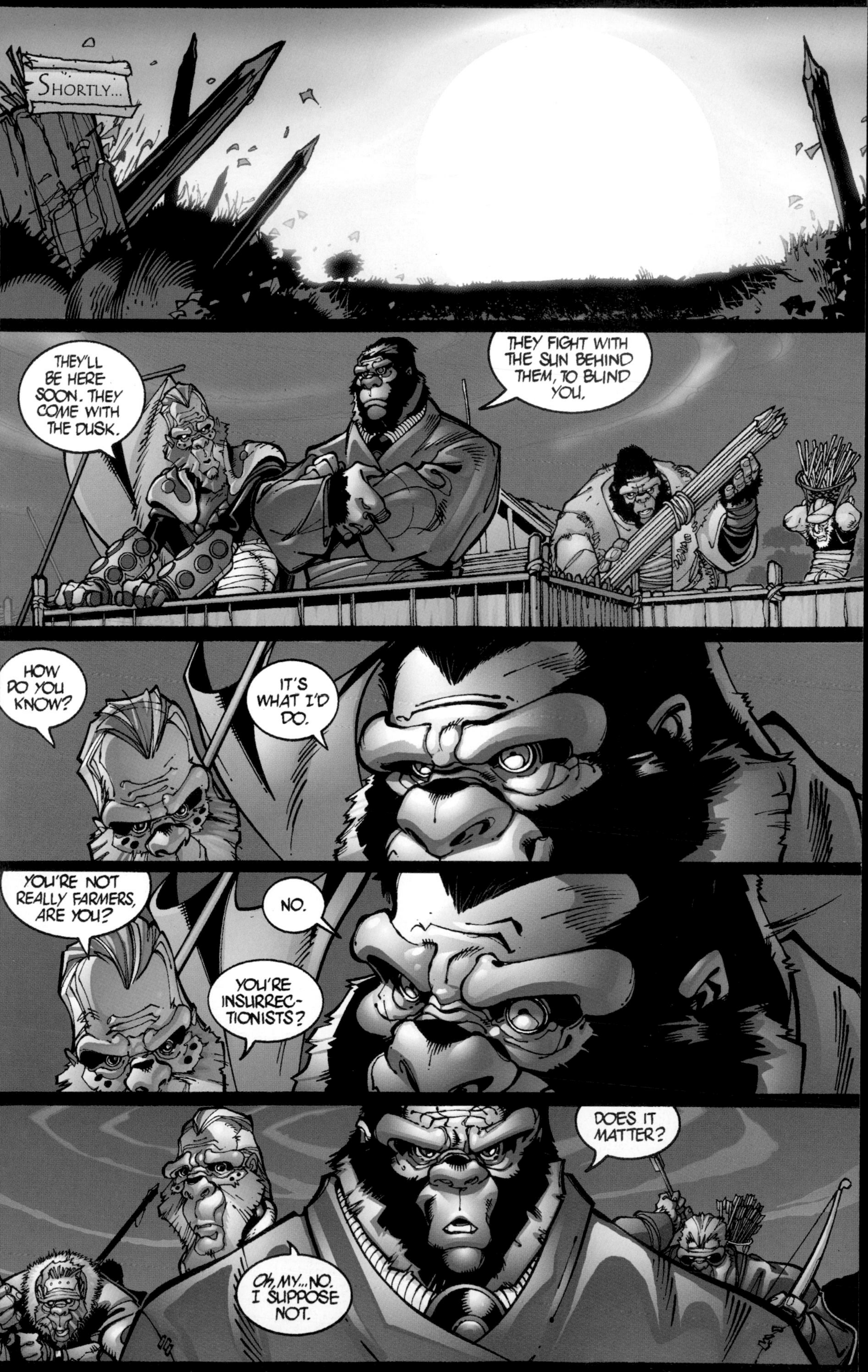
SHORTLY...
THEY'LL BE HERE SOON. THEY COME WITH THE DUSK.
THEY FIGHT WITH THE SUN BEHIND THEM, TO BLIND YOU.
HOW DO YOU KNOW?
IT'S WHAT I'D DO.
YOU'RE NOT REALLY FARMERS, ARE YOU?
NO.
YOU'RE INSURREC-TIONISTS?
DOES IT MATTER?
Oh, MY... NO. I SUPPOSE NOT.

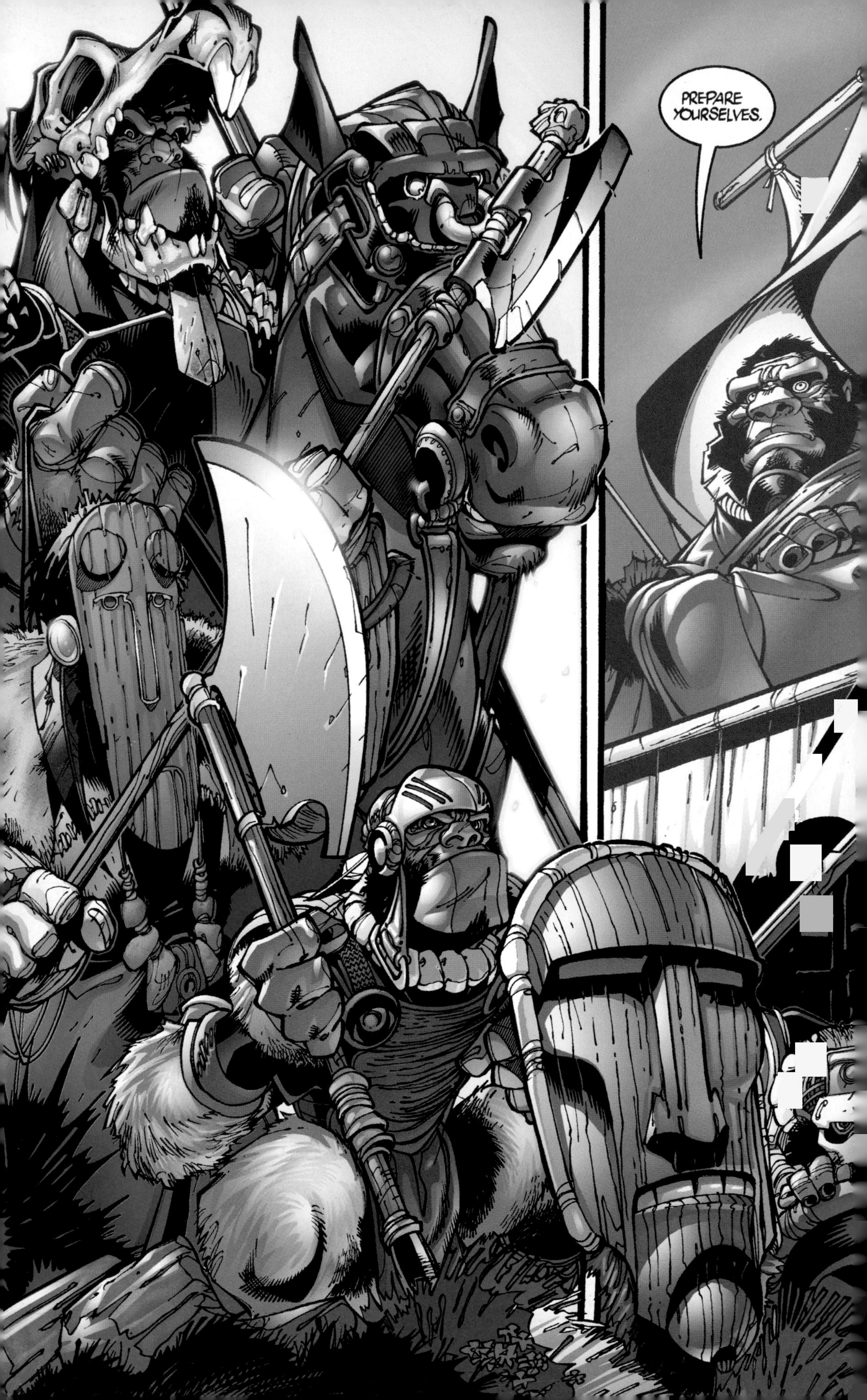
PREPARE YOURSELVES.

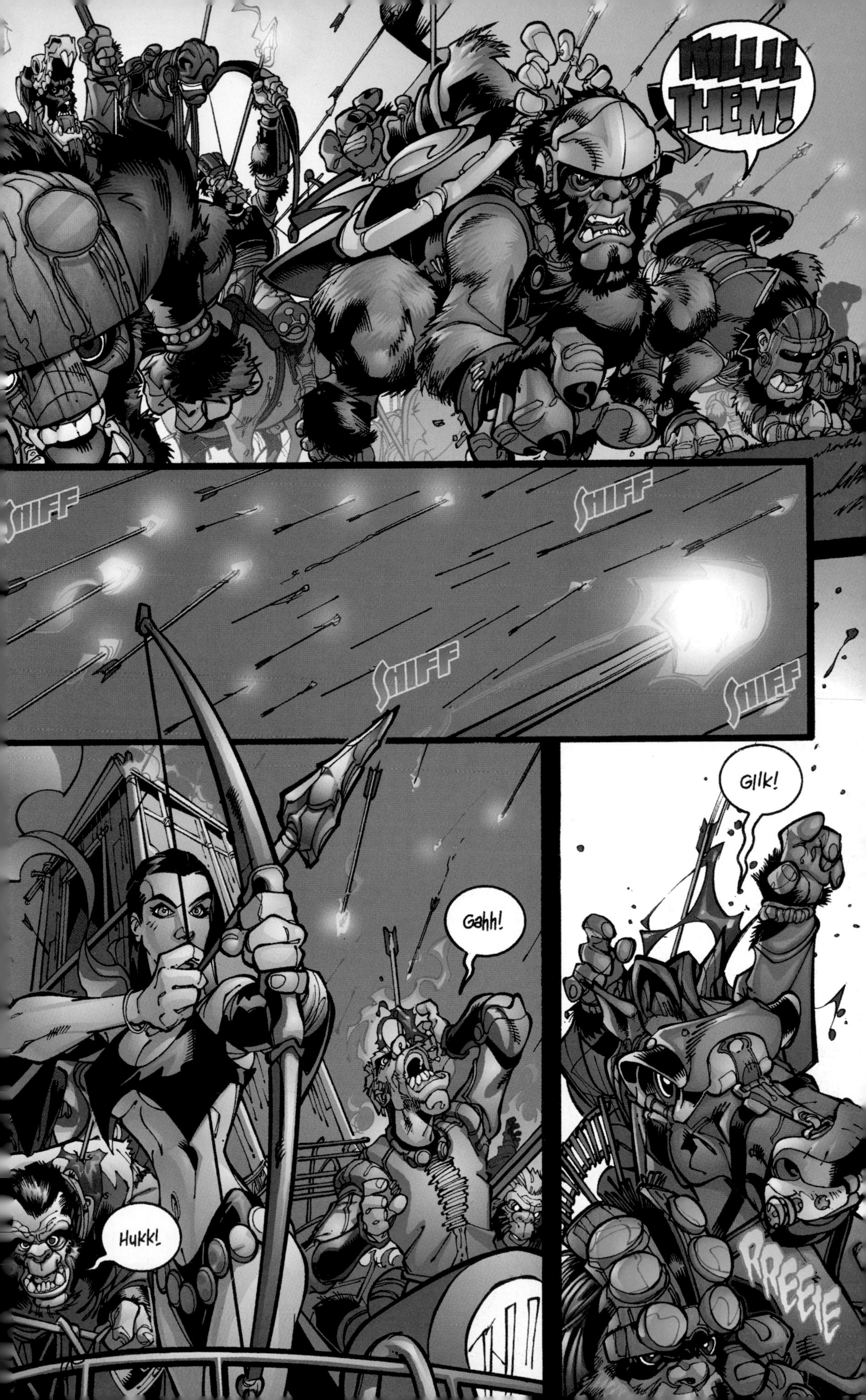
KILLLL THEM!
SHIFF
SHIFF
SHIFF
SHIFF
Gahh!
Hukk!
Glk!
RREEEE

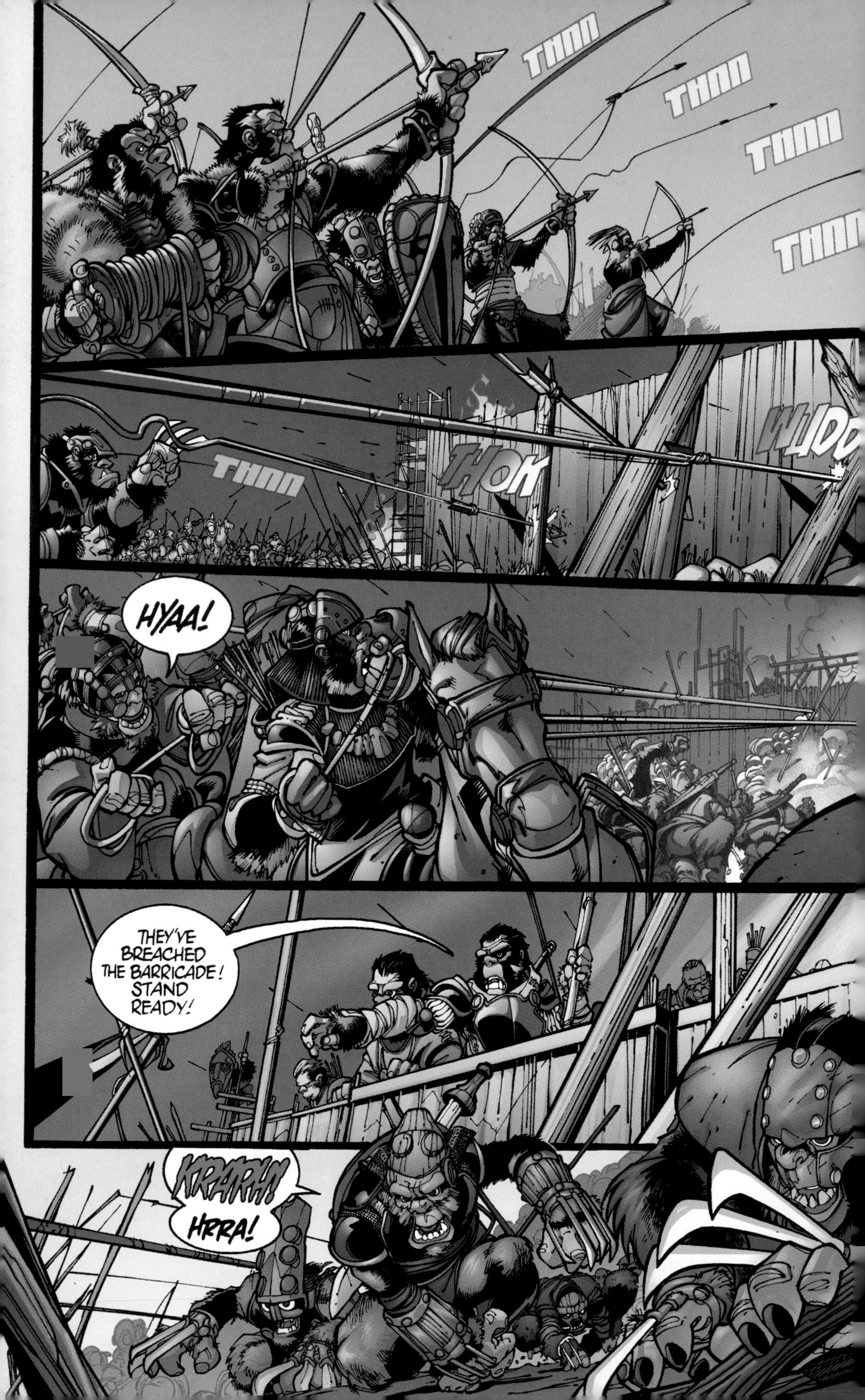
THNN
THNN
THNN
THNN
THNN
THOK
WUDD
HYAA!
THEY'VE BREACHED THE BARRICADE! STAND READY!
KRARH!
HRRA!

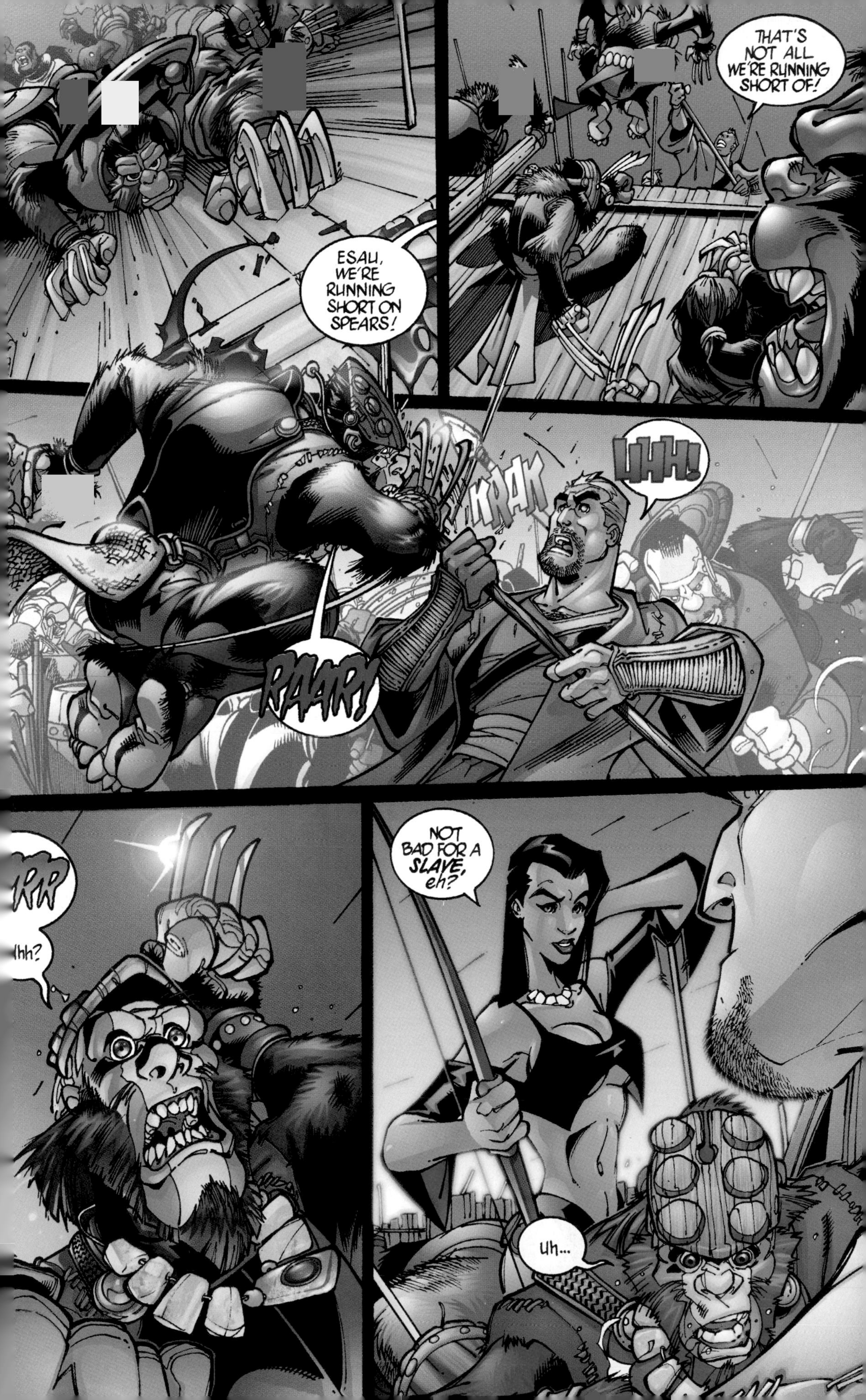
ESAU, WE'RE RUNNING SHORT ON SPEARS!
THAT'S NOT ALL WE'RE RUNNING SHORT OF!
KRAK
RAAAR!
UHH!
NOT BAD FOR A SLAVE, eh?
uh...

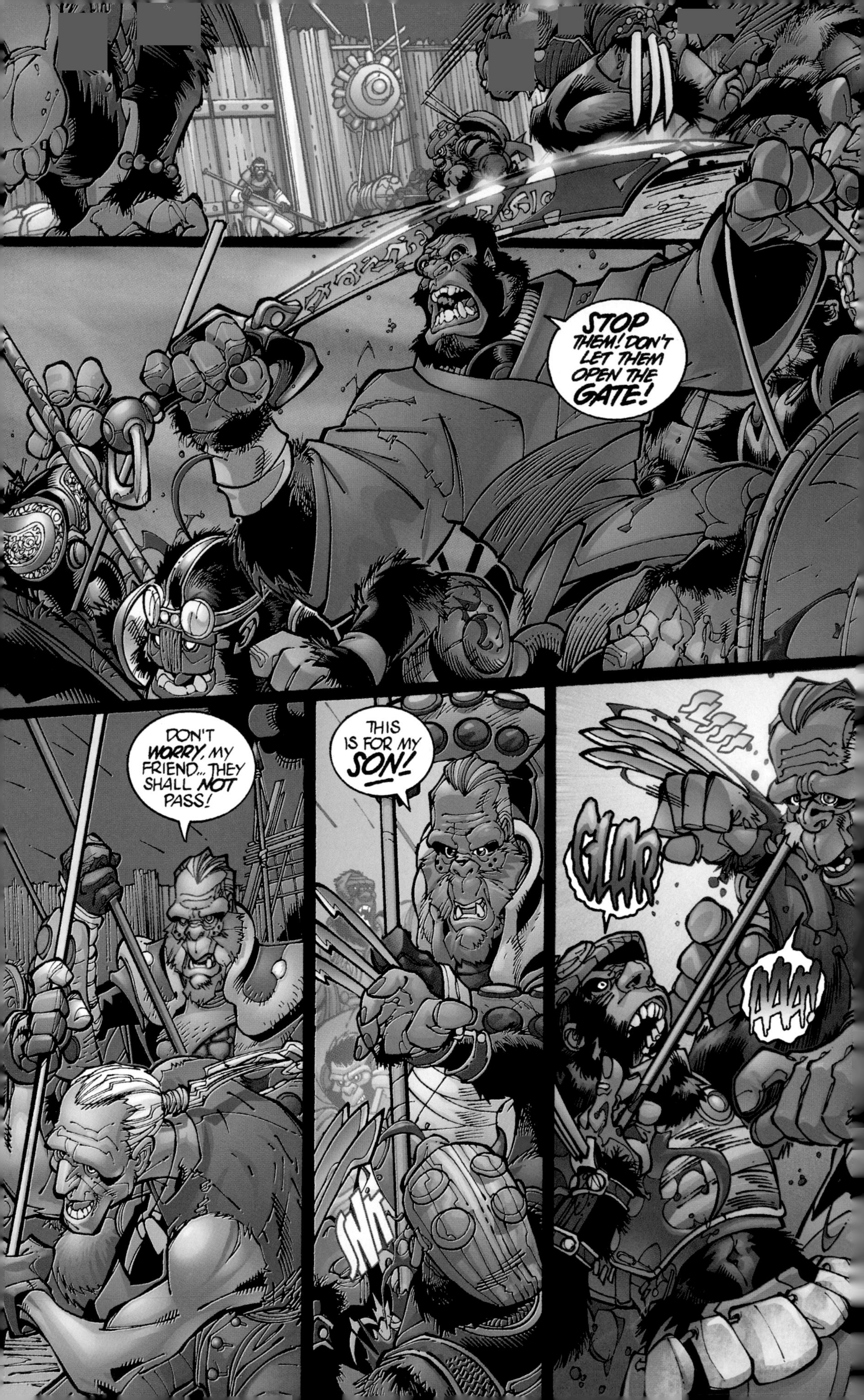
STOP THEM! DON'T LET THEM OPEN THE GATE!
DON'T WORRY, MY FRIEND... THEY SHALL NOT PASS!
THIS IS FOR MY SON!
GLAR
AAAH

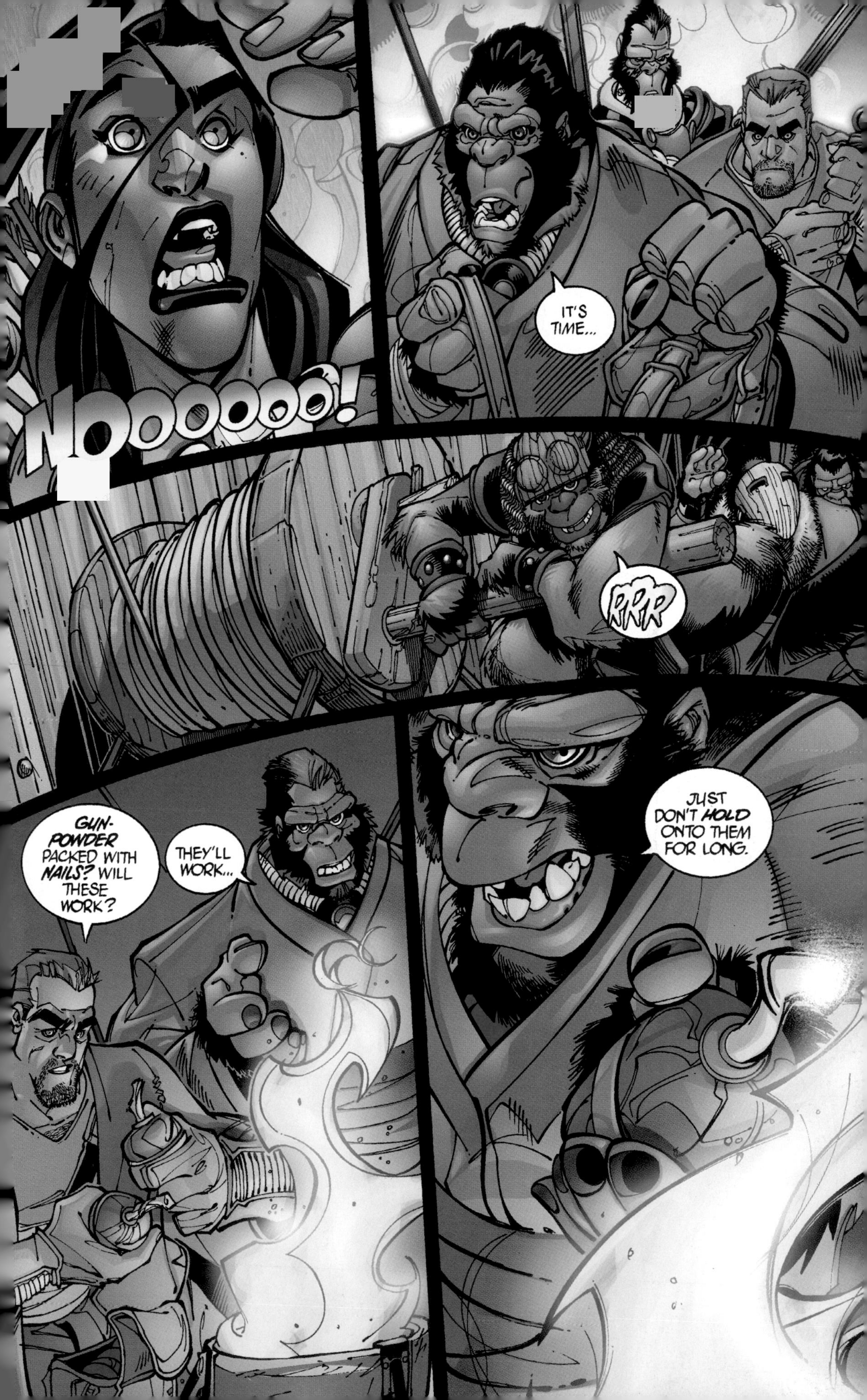
NOOOOOO!
IT'S TIME...
RRRR
GUN-POWDER PACKED WITH NAILS? WILL THESE WORK?
THEY'LL WORK...
JUST DON'T HOLD ONTO THEM FOR LONG.

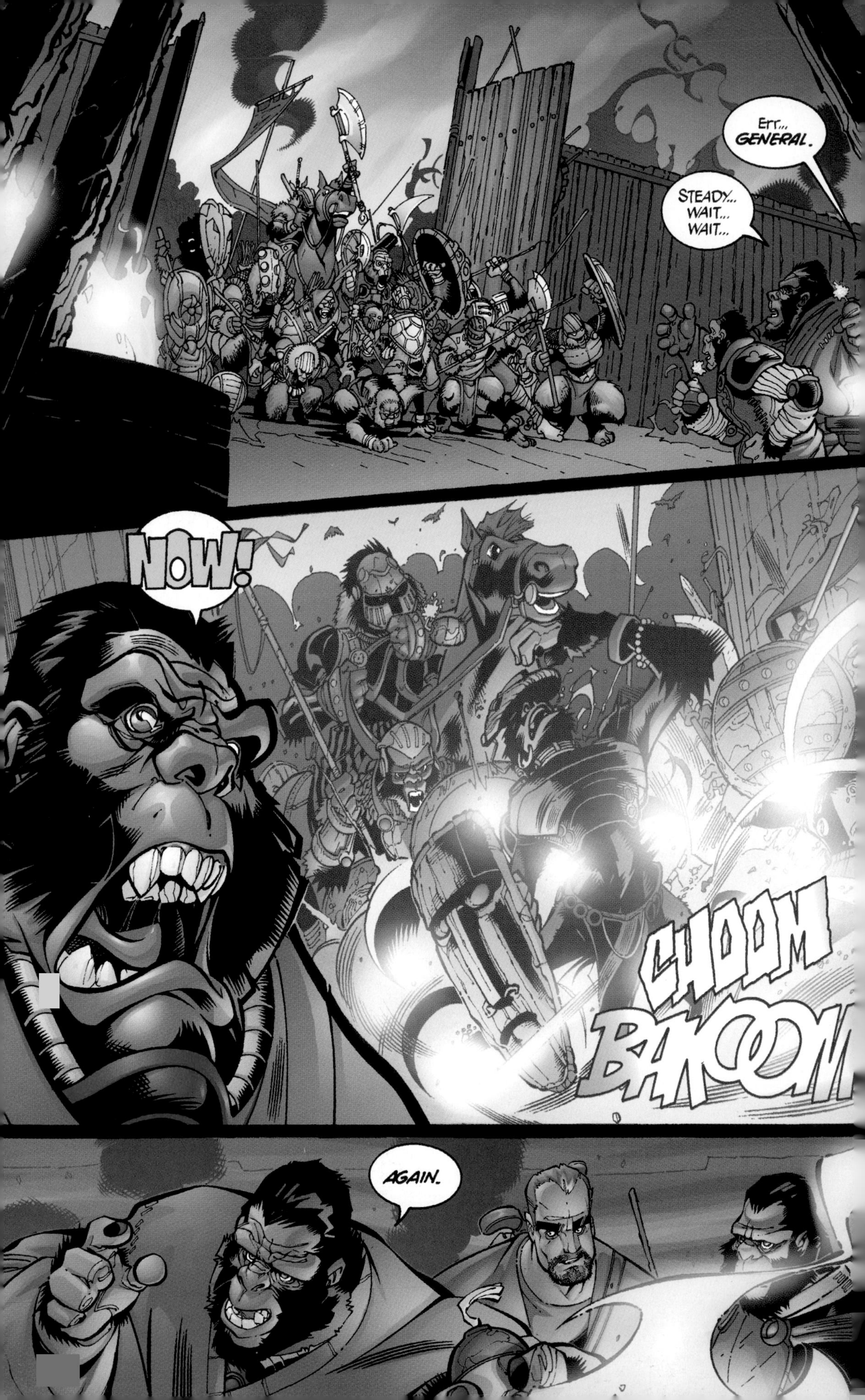
Err... GENERAL.
STEADY... WAIT... WAIT...
NOW!
CHOOM
BAROOM
AGAIN.

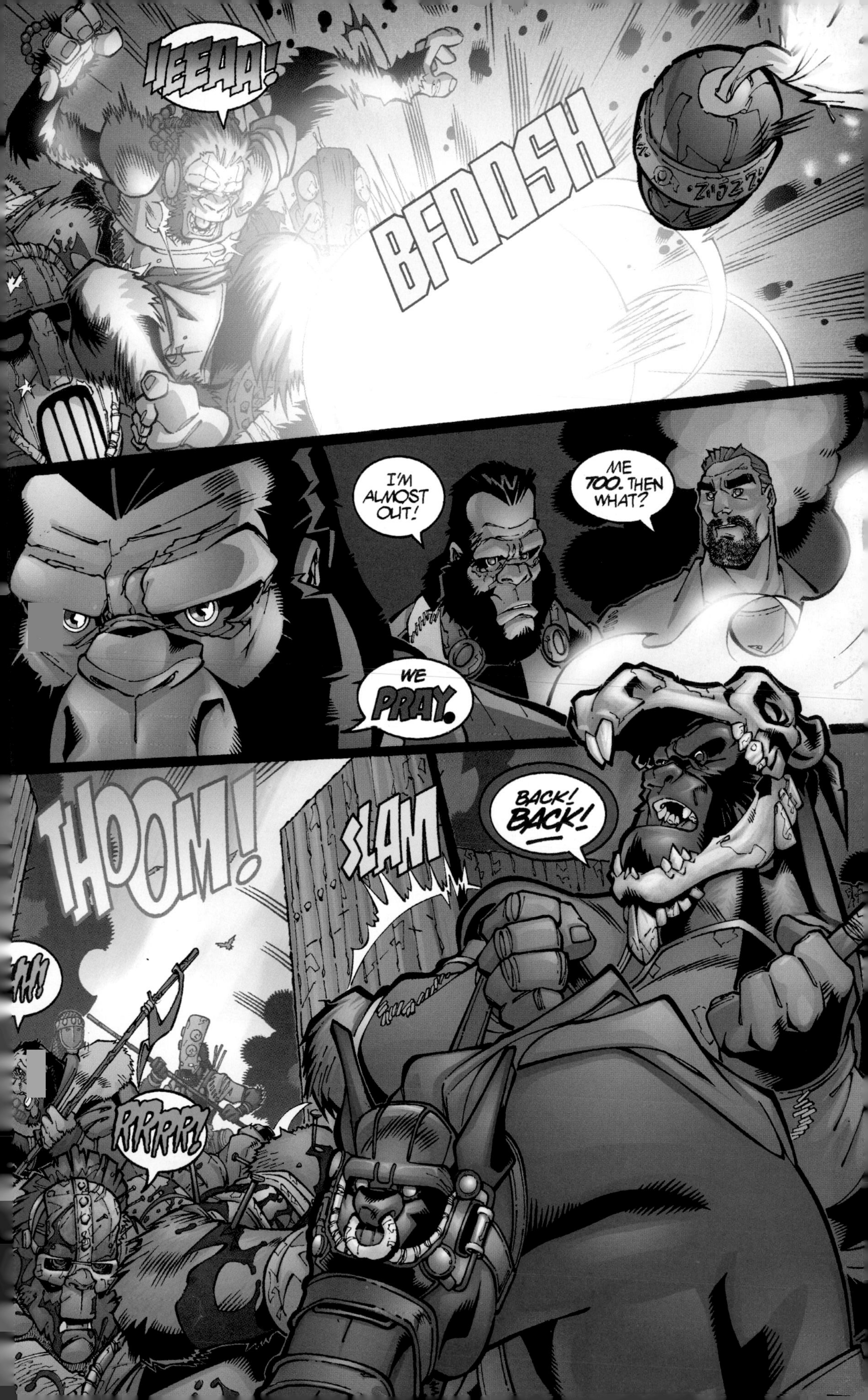

!IEEAA!
BFOOSH
I'M ALMOST OUT!
ME TOO. THEN WHAT?
WE PRAY.
THOOM!
SLAM
BACK! BACK!
RRRRRR!

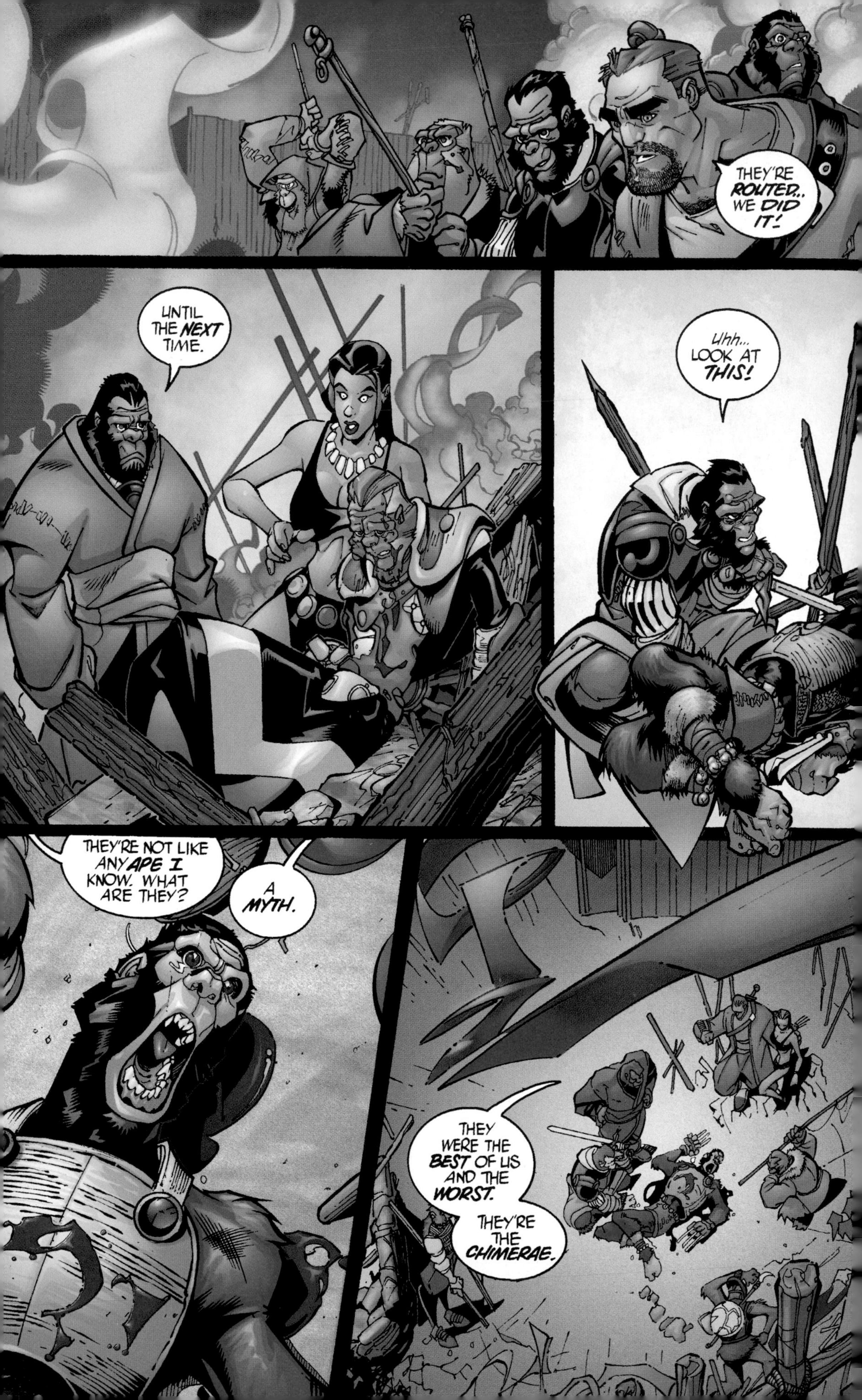
THEY'RE ROUTED... WE DID IT!
UNTIL THE NEXT TIME.
Uhh... LOOK AT THIS!
THEY'RE NOT LIKE ANY APE I KNOW. WHAT ARE THEY?
A MYTH.
THEY WERE THE BEST OF US AND THE WORST.
THEY'RE THE CHIMERAE.

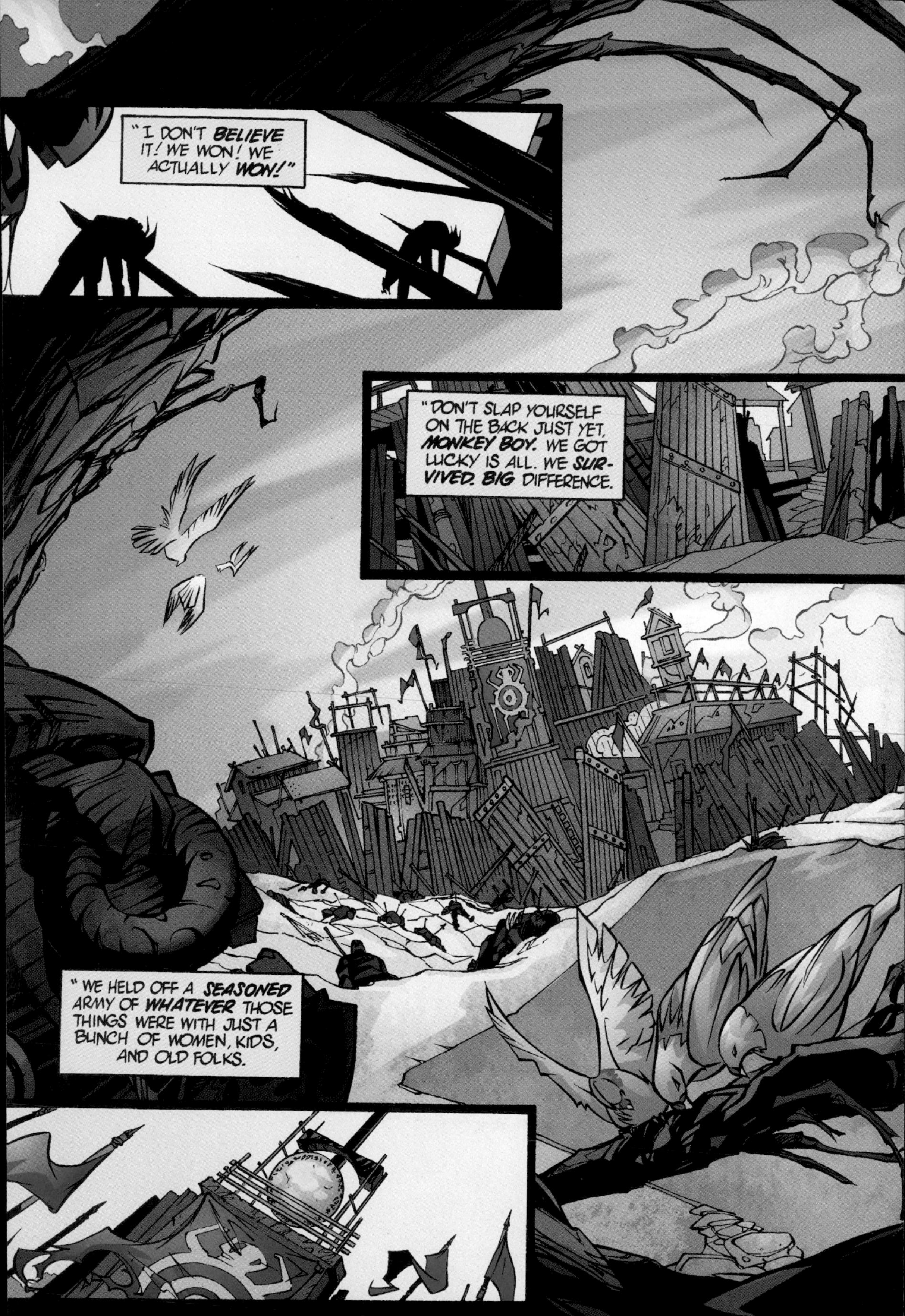
"I DON'T BELIEVE IT! WE WON! WE ACTUALLY WON!"
"DON'T SLAP YOURSELF ON THE BACK JUST YET, MONKEY BOY. WE GOT LUCKY IS ALL. WE SURVIVED. BIG DIFFERENCE.
"WE HELD OFF A SEASONED ARMY OF WHATEVER THOSE THINGS WERE WITH JUST A BUNCH OF WOMEN, KIDS, AND OLD FOLKS.

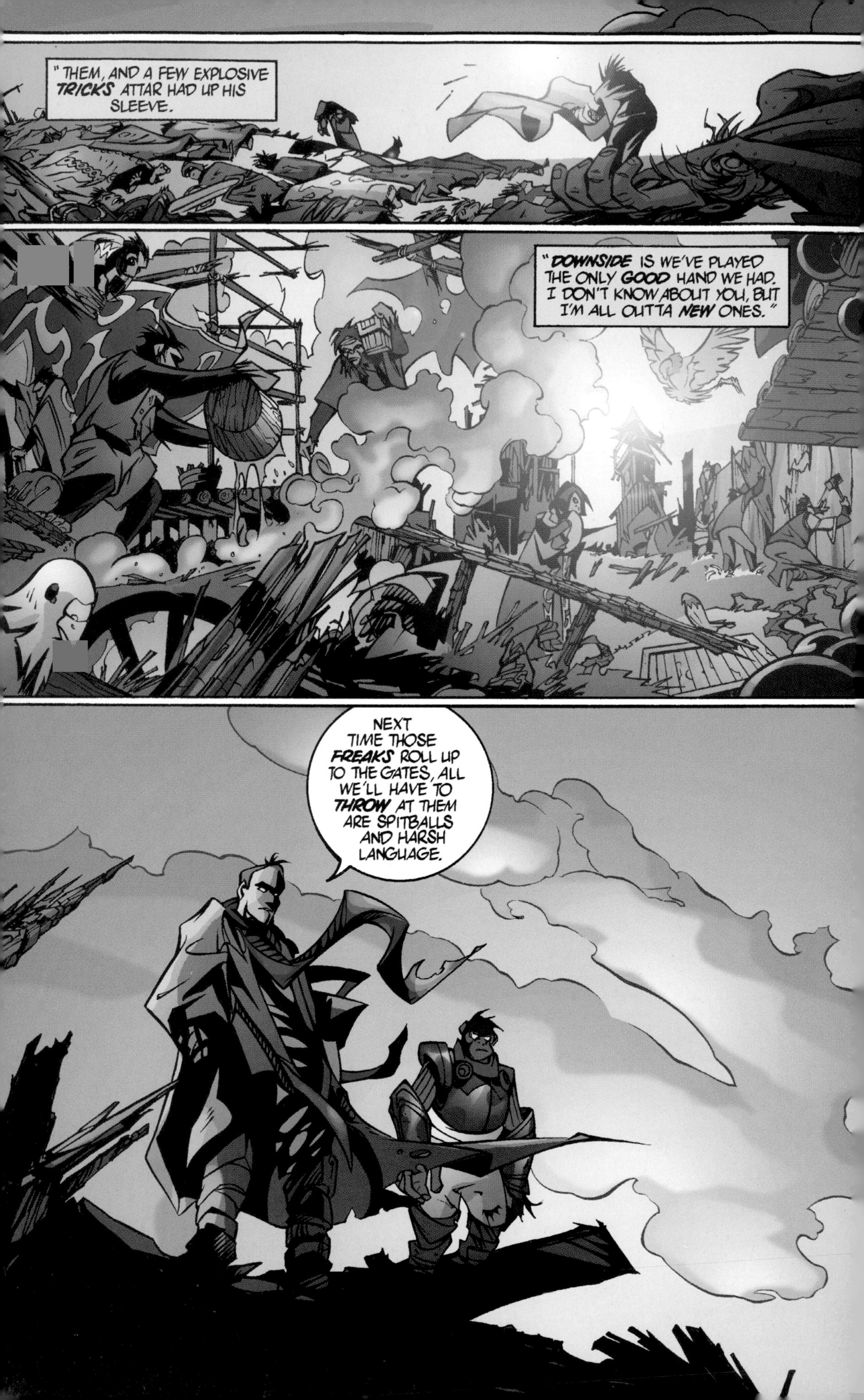
"THEM, AND A FEW EXPLOSIVE TRICKS ATTAR HAD UP HIS SLEEVE.
"DOWNSIDE IS WE'VE PLAYED THE ONLY GOOD HAND WE HAD. I DON'T KNOW ABOUT YOU, BUT I'M ALL OUTTA NEW ONES."
NEXT TIME THOSE FREAKS ROLL UP TO THE GATES, ALL WE'LL HAVE TO THROW AT THEM ARE SPITBALLS AND HARSH LANGUAGE.

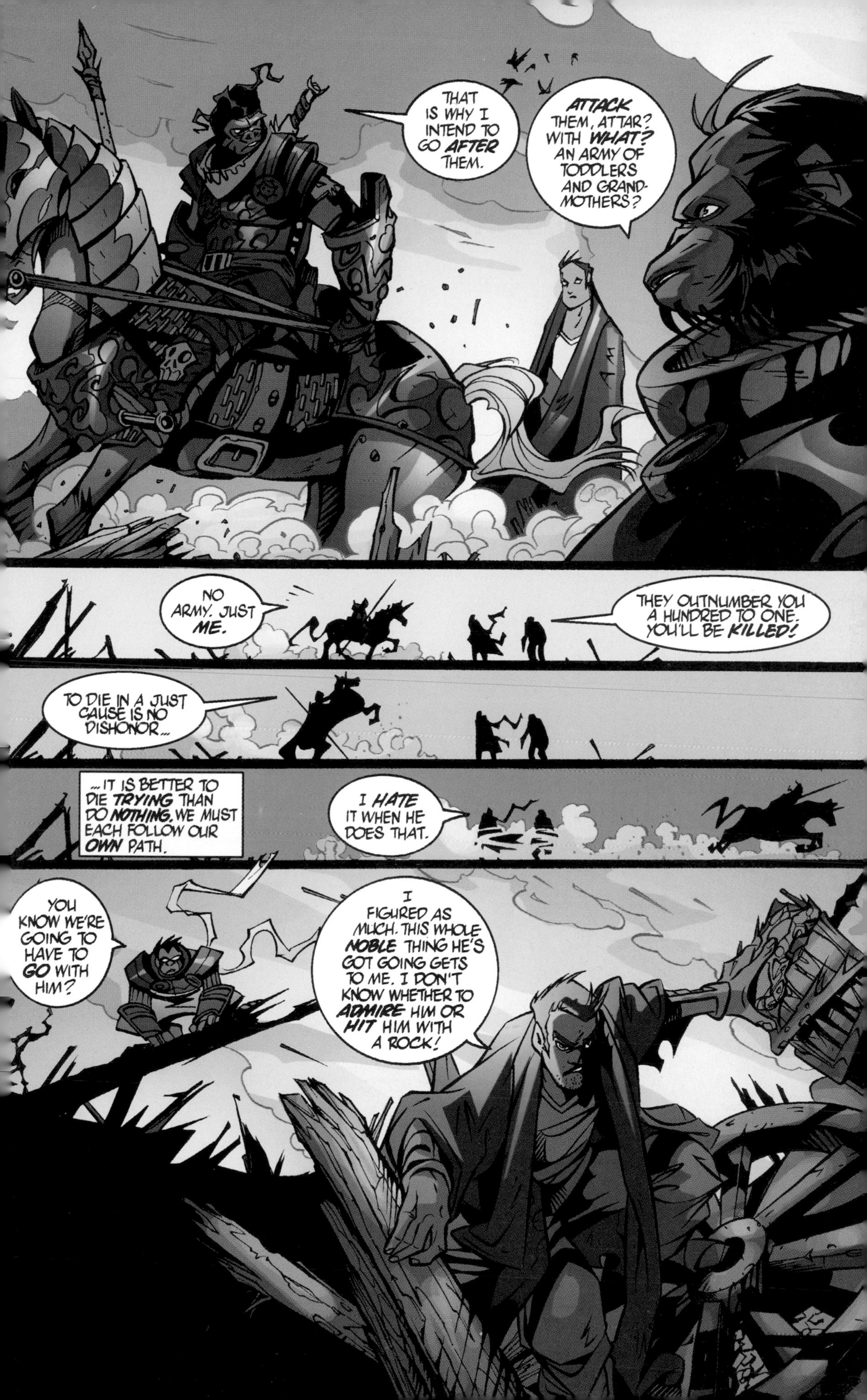
THAT IS WHY I INTEND TO GO AFTER THEM.
ATTACK THEM, ATTAR? WITH WHAT? AN ARMY OF TODDLERS AND GRAND-MOTHERS?
NO ARMY. JUST ME.
THEY OUTNUMBER YOU A HUNDRED TO ONE. YOU'LL BE KILLED!
TO DIE IN A JUST CAUSE IS NO DISHONOR...
...IT IS BETTER TO DIE TRYING THAN DO NOTHING. WE MUST EACH FOLLOW OUR OWN PATH.
I HATE IT WHEN HE DOES THAT.
YOU KNOW WE'RE GOING TO HAVE TO GO WITH HIM?
I FIGURED AS MUCH. THIS WHOLE NOBLE THING HE'S GOT GOING GETS TO ME. I DON'T KNOW WHETHER TO ADMIRE HIM OR HIT HIM WITH A ROCK!

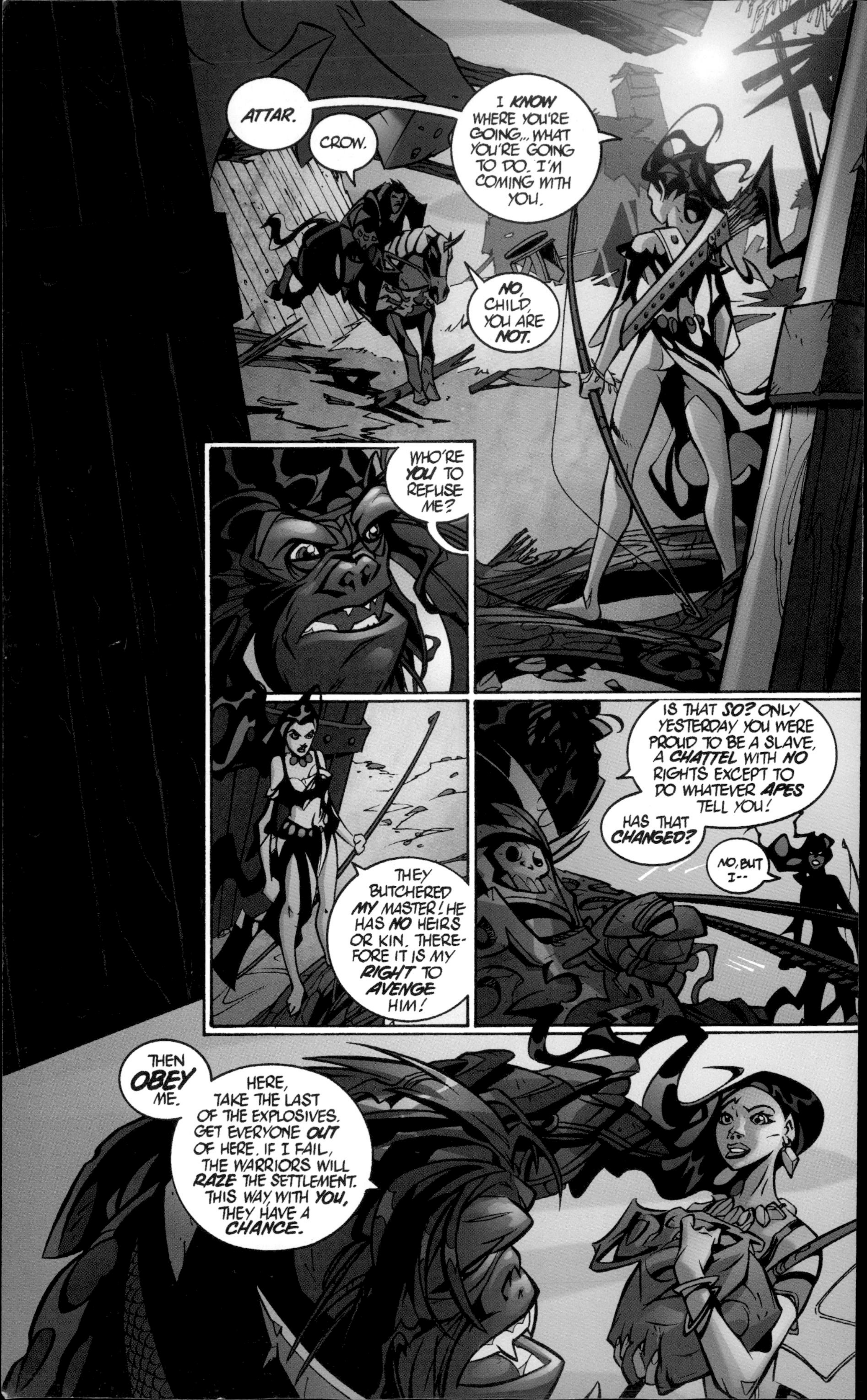
ATTAR.
CROW.
I KNOW WHERE YOU'RE GOING... WHAT YOU'RE GOING TO DO. I'M COMING WITH YOU.
NO, CHILD, YOU ARE NOT.
WHO'RE YOU TO REFUSE ME?
THEY BUTCHERED MY MASTER! HE HAS NO HEIRS OR KIN. THEREFORE IT IS MY RIGHT TO AVENGE HIM!
IS THAT SO? ONLY YESTERDAY YOU WERE PROUD TO BE A SLAVE, A CHATTEL WITH NO RIGHTS EXCEPT TO DO WHATEVER APES TELL YOU!
HAS THAT CHANGED?
NO, BUT I--
THEN OBEY ME.
HERE, TAKE THE LAST OF THE EXPLOSIVES. GET EVERYONE OUT OF HERE. IF I FAIL, THE WARRIORS WILL RAZE THE SETTLEMENT. THIS WAY, WITH YOU, THEY HAVE A CHANCE.

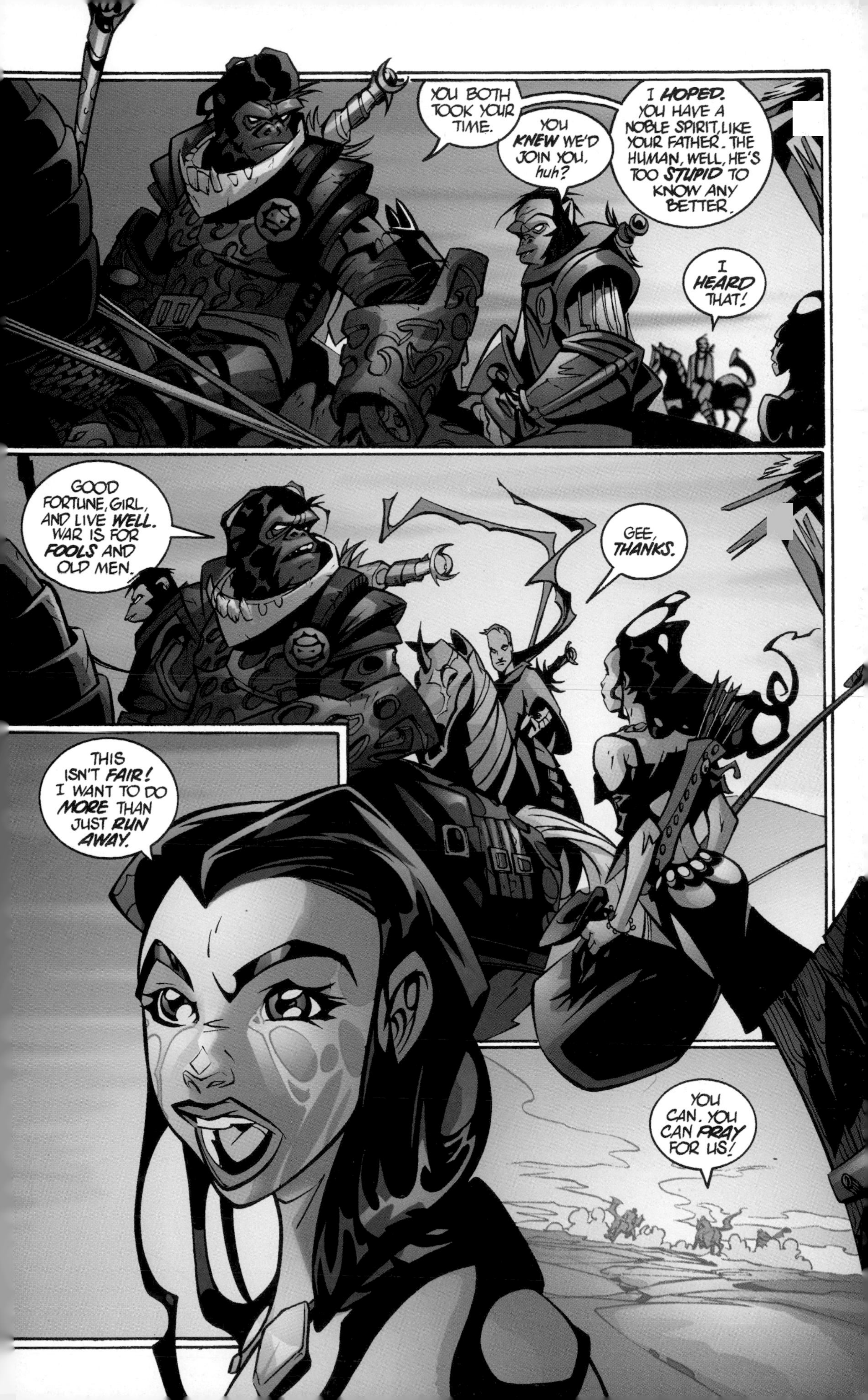

YOU BOTH TOOK YOUR TIME.
YOU KNEW WE'D JOIN YOU, huh?
I HOPED. YOU HAVE A NOBLE SPIRIT, LIKE YOUR FATHER. THE HUMAN, WELL, HE'S TOO STUPID TO KNOW ANY BETTER.
I HEARD THAT!
GOOD FORTUNE, GIRL, AND LIVE WELL. WAR IS FOR FOOLS AND OLD MEN.
GEE, THANKS.
THIS ISN'T FAIR! I WANT TO DO MORE THAN JUST RUN AWAY.
YOU CAN. YOU CAN PRAY FOR US!

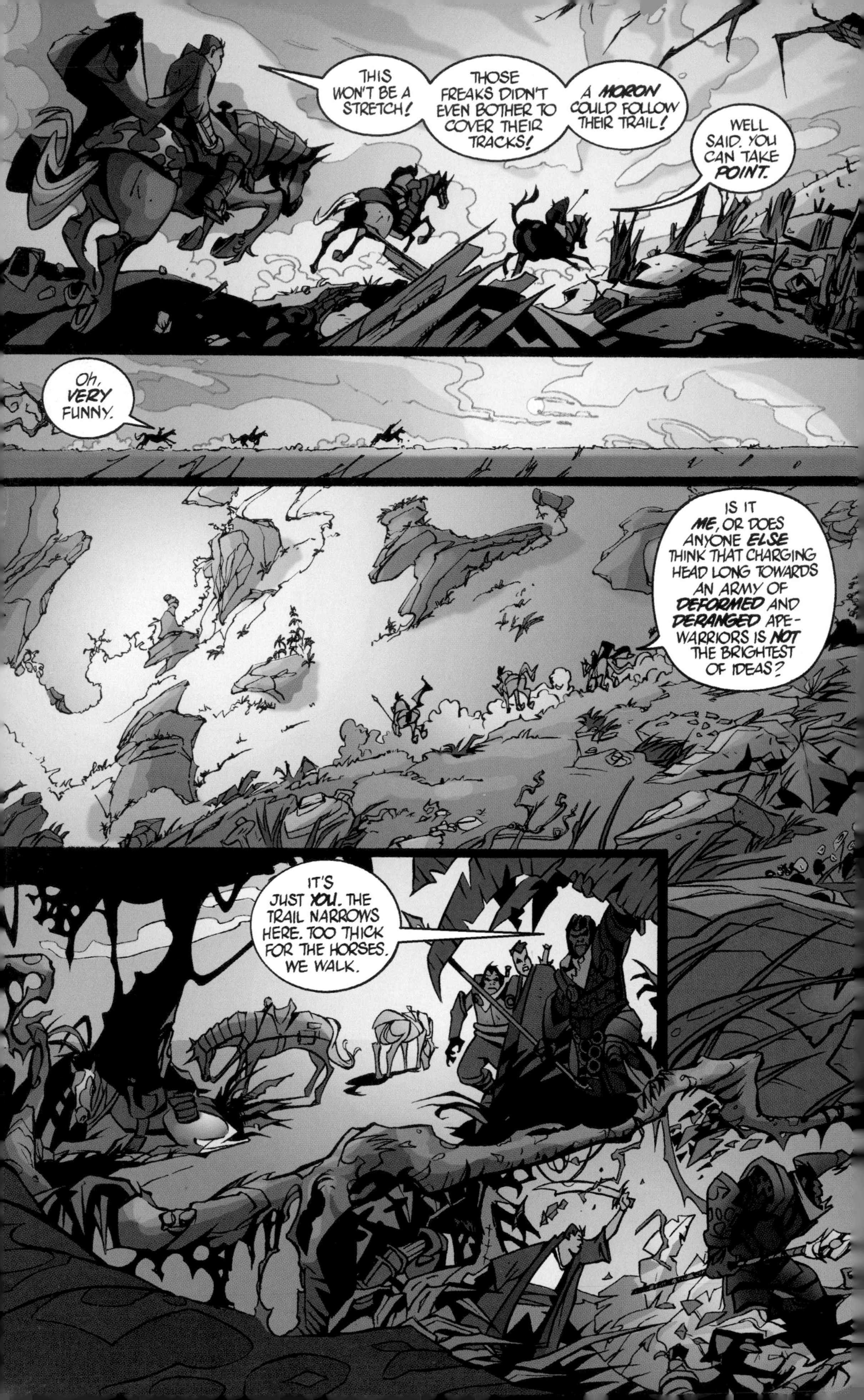
THIS WON'T BE A STRETCH!
THOSE FREAKS DIDN'T EVEN BOTHER TO COVER THEIR TRACKS!
A MORON COULD FOLLOW THEIR TRAIL!
WELL SAID. YOU CAN TAKE POINT.
Oh, VERY FUNNY.
IS IT ME, OR DOES ANYONE ELSE THINK THAT CHARGING HEAD LONG TOWARDS AN ARMY OF DEFORMED AND DERANGED APE-WARRIORS IS NOT THE BRIGHTEST OF IDEAS?
IT'S JUST YOU. THE TRAIL NARROWS HERE. TOO THICK FOR THE HORSES. WE WALK.

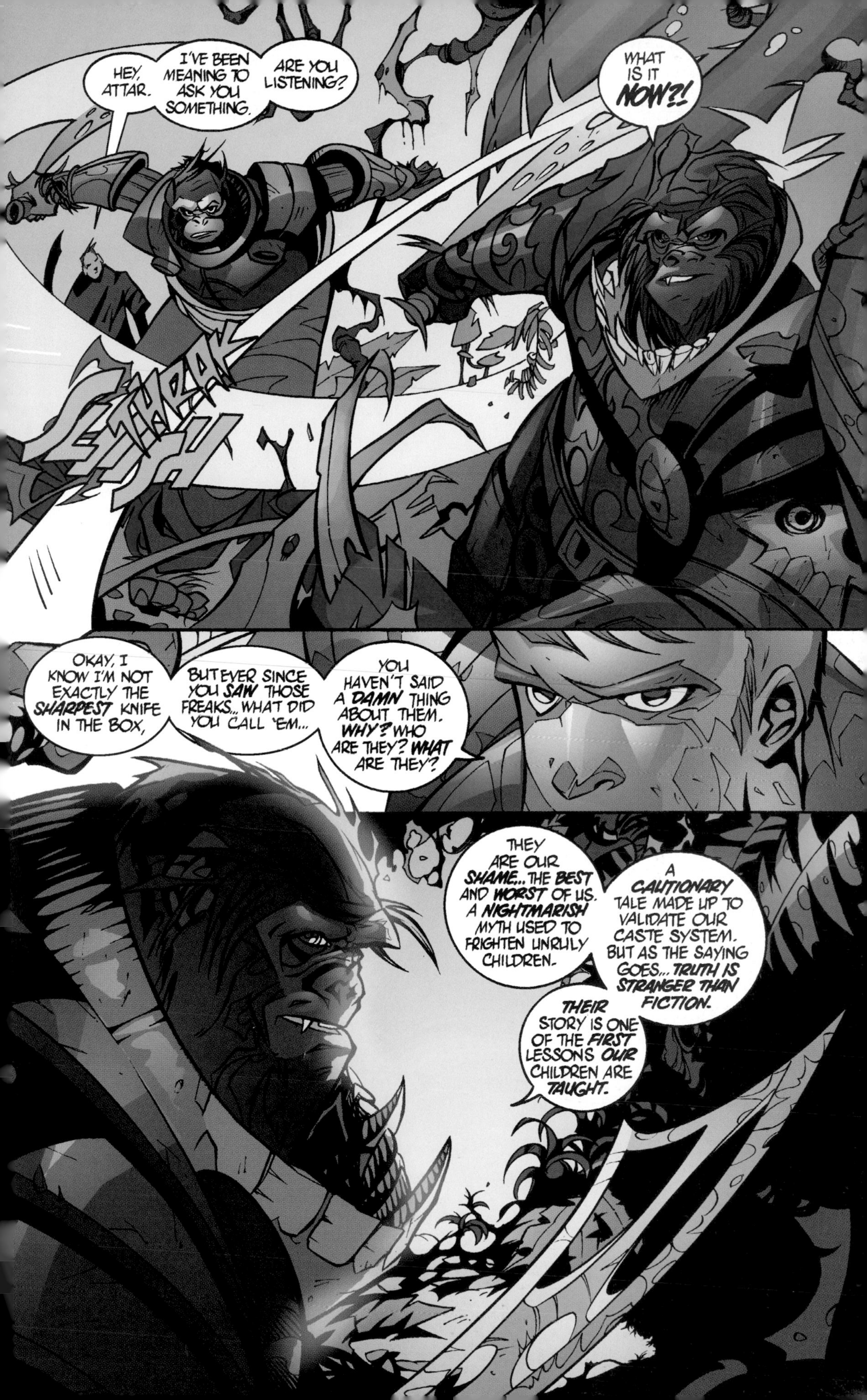
HEY, ATTAR.
I'VE BEEN MEANING TO ASK YOU SOMETHING.
ARE YOU LISTENING?
WHAT IS IT NOW?!
THRAK
SHUNK
OKAY, I KNOW I'M NOT EXACTLY THE SHARPEST KNIFE IN THE BOX,
BUT EVER SINCE YOU SAW THOSE FREAKS... WHAT DID YOU CALL 'EM...
YOU HAVEN'T SAID A DAMN THING ABOUT THEM. WHY? WHO ARE THEY? WHAT ARE THEY?
THEY ARE OUR SHAME... THE BEST AND WORST OF US. A NIGHTMARISH MYTH USED TO FRIGHTEN UNRULY CHILDREN.
A CAUTIONARY TALE MADE UP TO VALIDATE OUR CASTE SYSTEM. BUT AS THE SAYING GOES... TRUTH IS STRANGER THAN FICTION.
THEIR STORY IS ONE OF THE FIRST LESSONS OUR CHILDREN ARE TAUGHT.

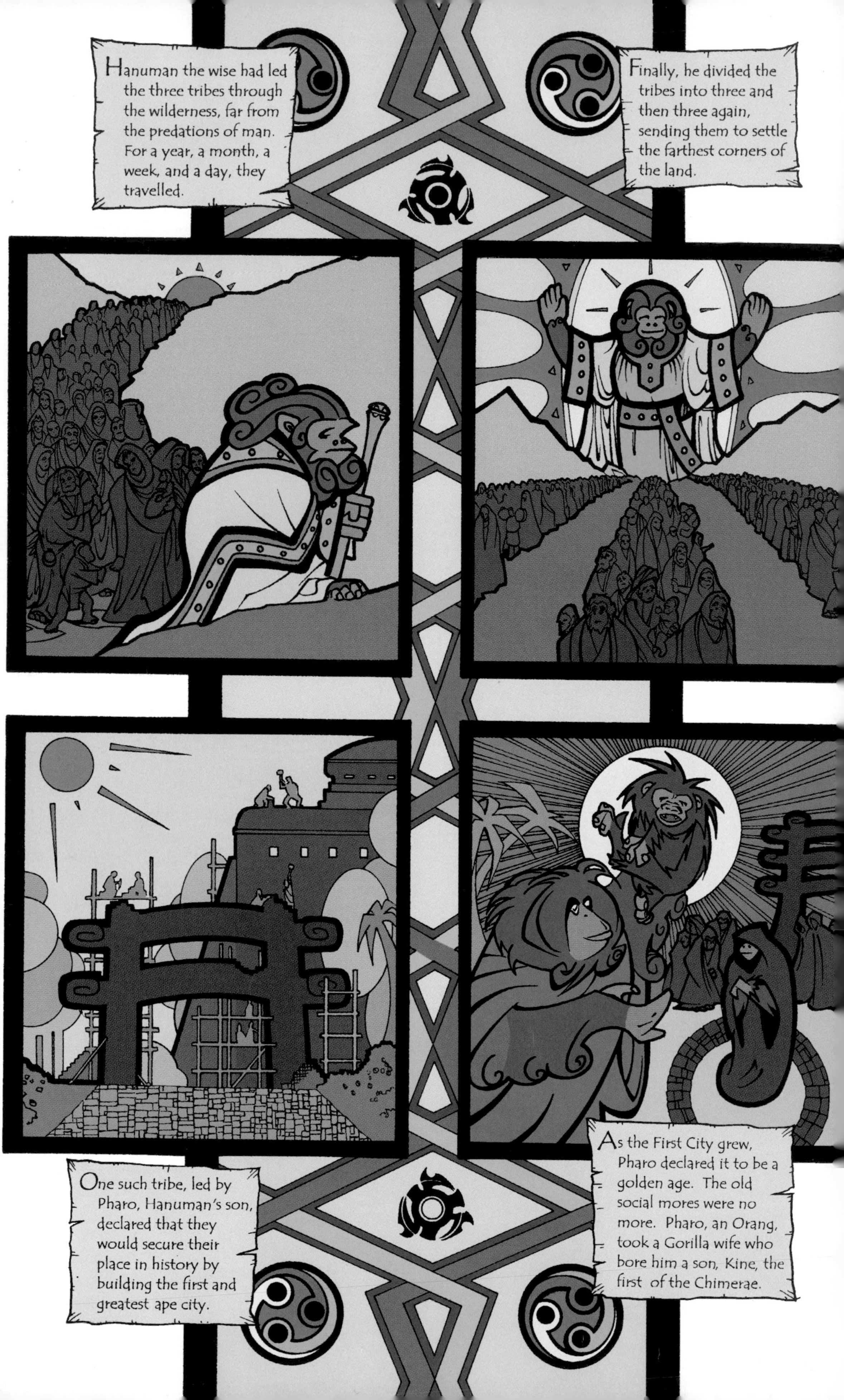
Hanuman the wise had led the three tribes through the wilderness, far from the predations of man. For a year, a month, a week, and a day, they travelled.
Finally, he divided the tribes into three and then three again, sending them to settle the farthest corners of the land.
One such tribe, led by Pharo, Hanuman's son, declared that they would secure their place in history by building the first and greatest ape city.
As the First City grew, Pharo declared it to be a golden age. The old social mores were no more. Pharo, an Orang, took a Gorilla wife who bore him a son, Kine, the first of the Chimerae.

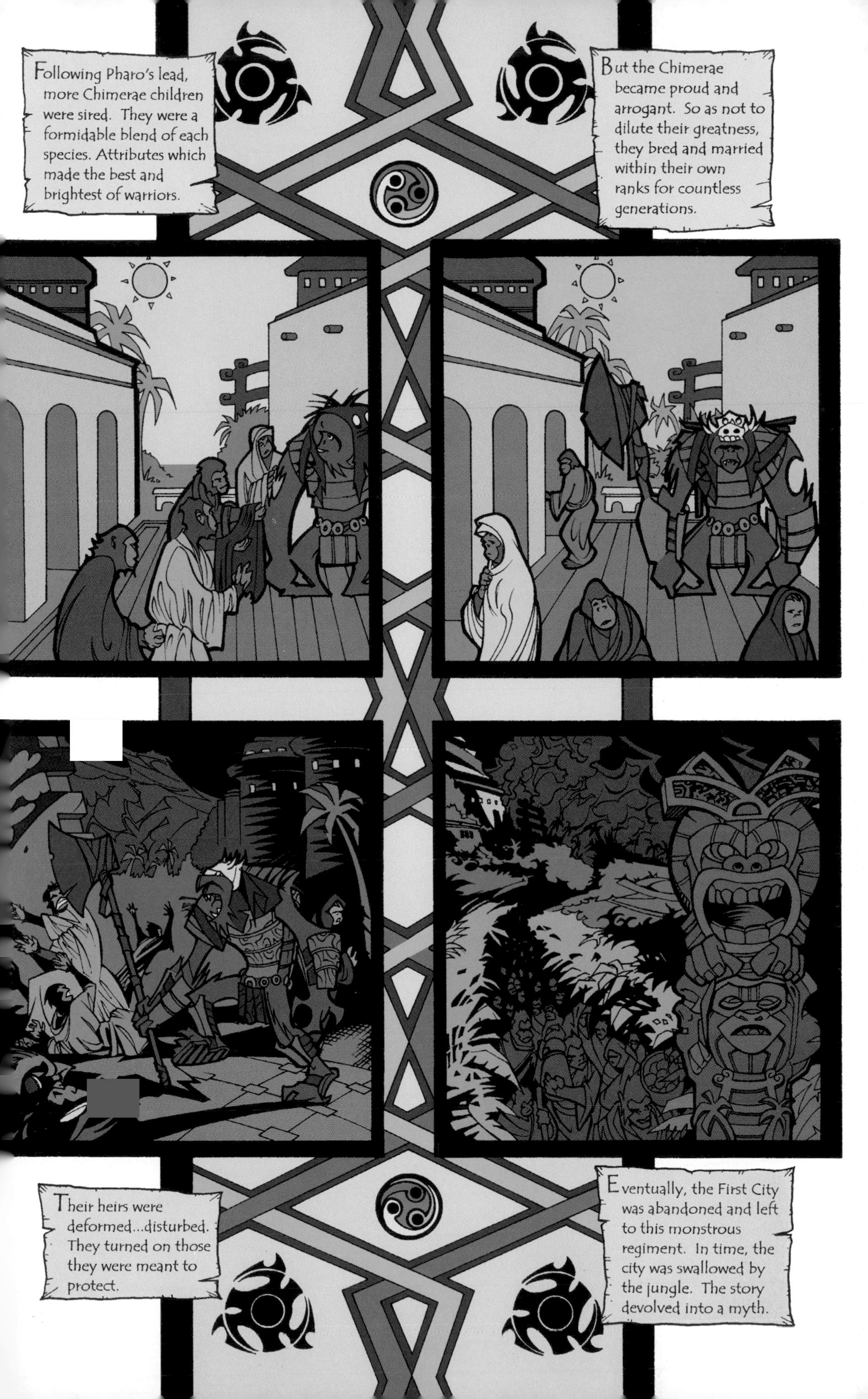
Following Pharo's lead, more Chimerae children were sired. They were a formidable blend of each species. Attributes which made the best and brightest of warriors.
But the Chimerae became proud and arrogant. So as not to dilute their greatness, they bred and married within their own ranks for countless generations.
Their heirs were deformed...disturbed. They turned on those they were meant to protect.
Eventually, the First City was abandoned and left to this monstrous regiment. In time, the city was swallowed by the jungle. The story devolved into a myth.

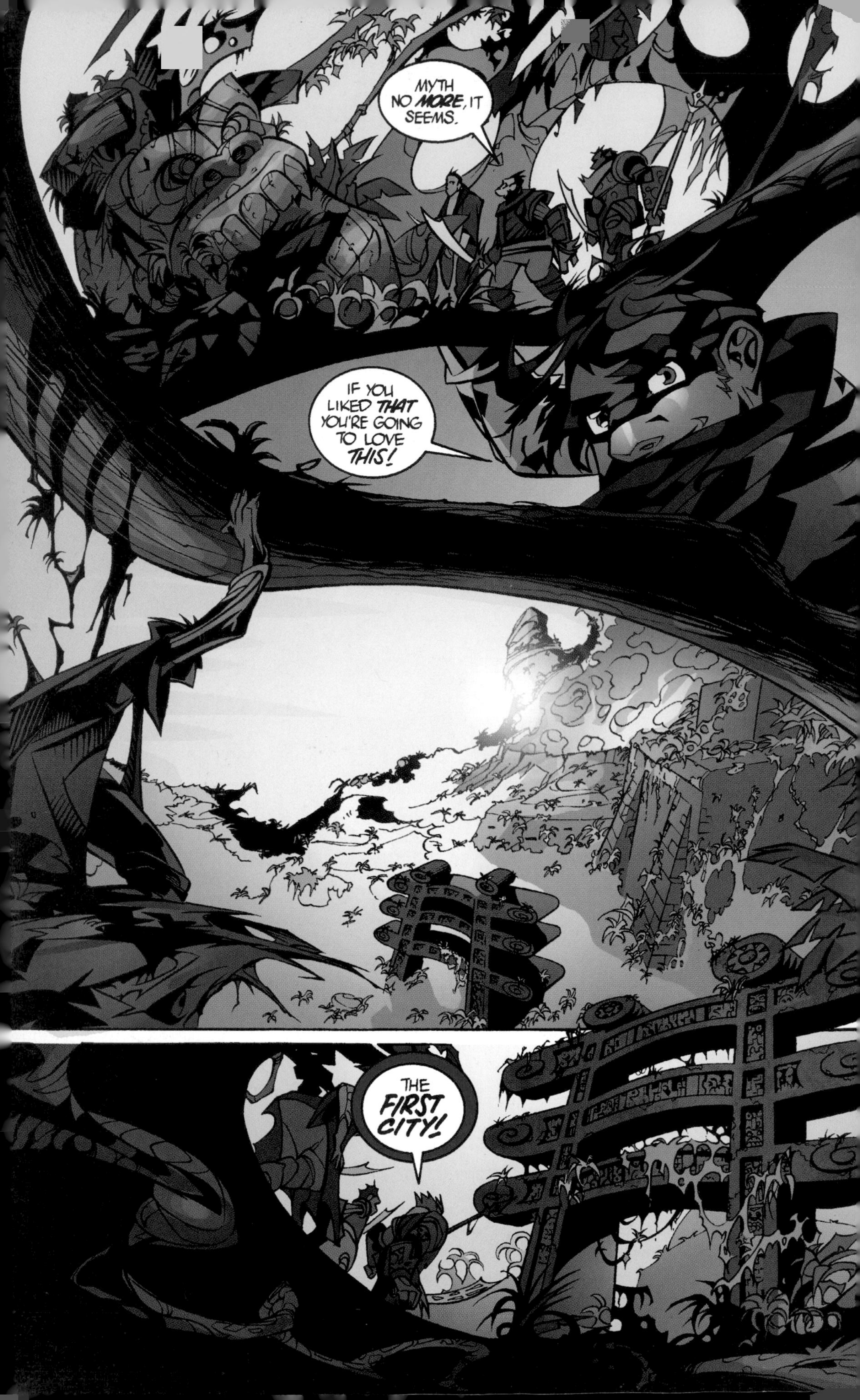
MYTH NO MORE, IT SEEMS.
IF YOU LIKED THAT YOU'RE GOING TO LOVE THIS!
THE FIRST CITY!

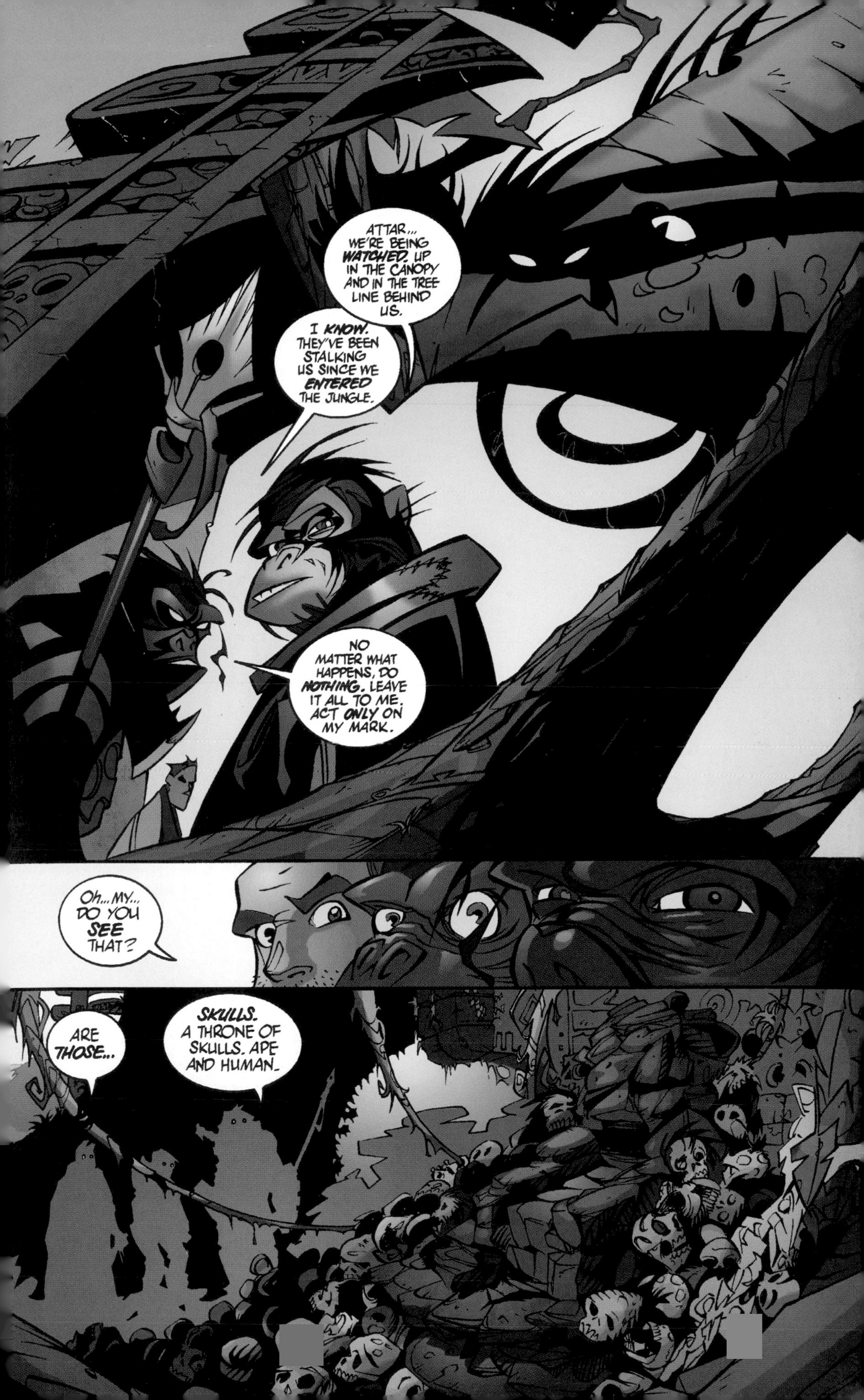
ATTAR... WE'RE BEING WATCHED. UP IN THE CANOPY AND IN THE TREE LINE BEHIND US.
I KNOW. THEY'VE BEEN STALKING US SINCE WE ENTERED THE JUNGLE.
NO MATTER WHAT HAPPENS, DO NOTHING. LEAVE IT ALL TO ME. ACT ONLY ON MY MARK.
Oh... MY... DO YOU SEE THAT?
ARE THOSE...
SKULLS. A THRONE OF SKULLS. APE AND HUMAN.

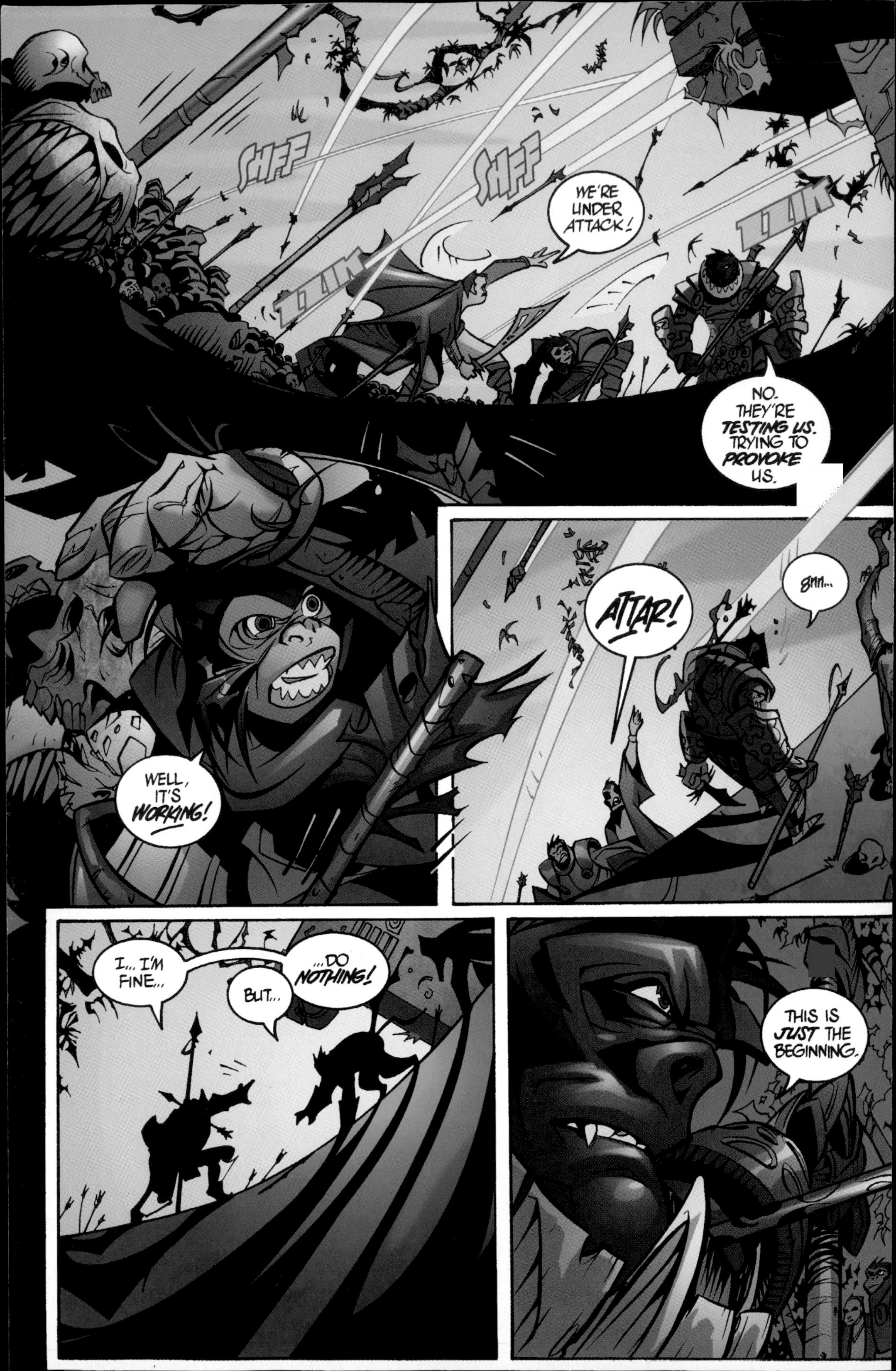
SHFF
SHFF
WE'RE UNDER ATTACK!
ZZZIN
ZZZIN
NO. THEY'RE TESTING US. TRYING TO PROVOKE US.
WELL, IT'S WORKING!
ATTAR!
GNN...
I... I'M FINE...
BUT...
...DO NOTHING!
THIS IS JUST THE BEGINNING.

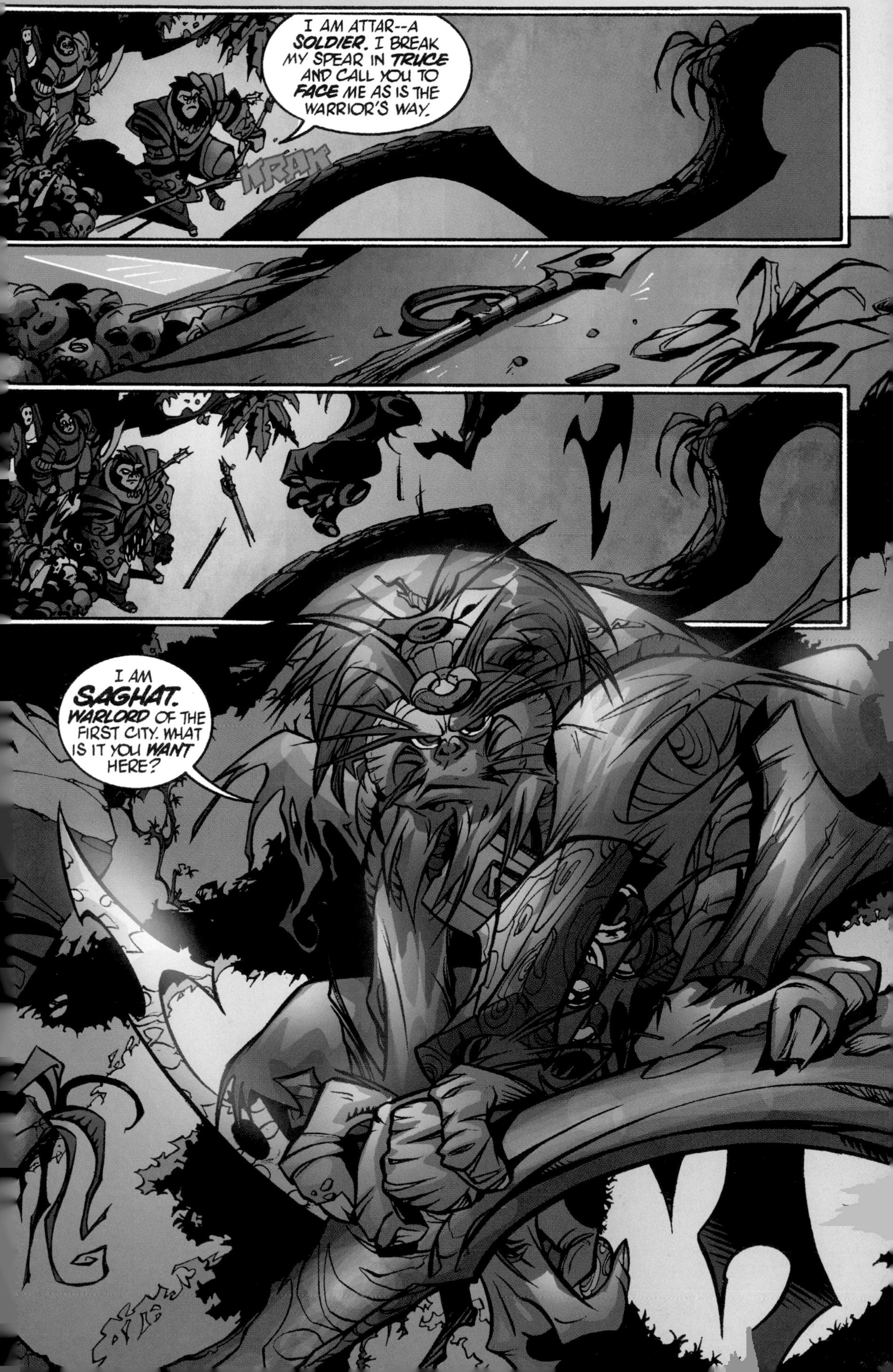
I AM ATTAR--A SOLDIER. I BREAK MY SPEAR IN TRUCE AND CALL YOU TO FACE ME AS IS THE WARRIOR'S WAY.
KRAK
I AM SAGHAT. WARLORD OF THE FIRST CITY. WHAT IS IT YOU WANT HERE?

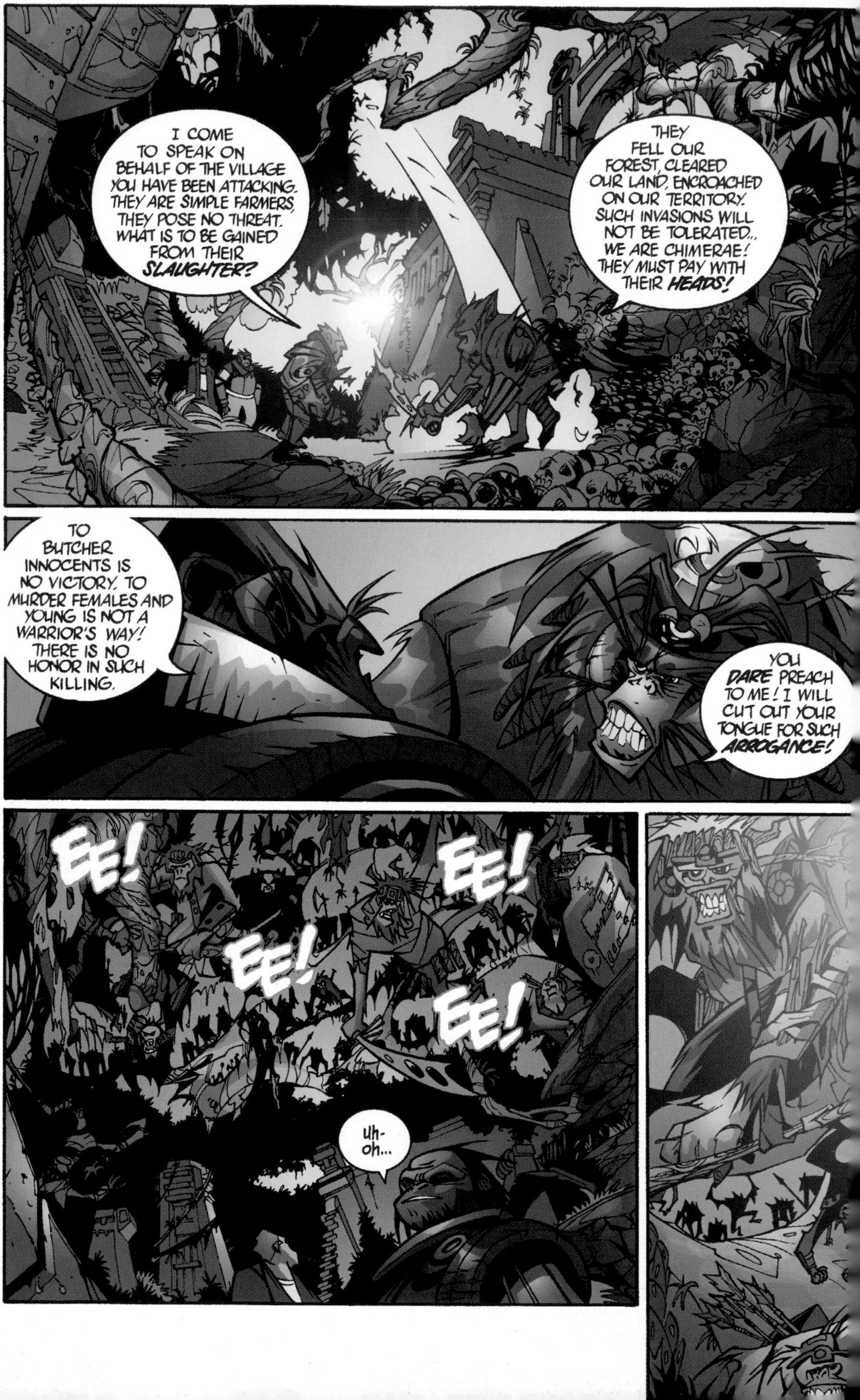
I COME TO SPEAK ON BEHALF OF THE VILLAGE YOU HAVE BEEN ATTACKING. THEY ARE SIMPLE FARMERS, THEY POSE NO THREAT. WHAT IS TO BE GAINED FROM THEIR SLAUGHTER?
THEY FELL OUR FOREST, CLEARED OUR LAND, ENCROACHED ON OUR TERRITORY. SUCH INVASIONS WILL NOT BE TOLERATED... WE ARE CHIMERAE! THEY MUST PAY WITH THEIR HEADS!
TO BUTCHER INNOCENTS IS NO VICTORY. TO MURDER FEMALES AND YOUNG IS NOT A WARRIOR'S WAY! THERE IS NO HONOR IN SUCH KILLING.
YOU DARE PREACH TO ME! I WILL CUT OUT YOUR TONGUE FOR SUCH ARROGANCE!
EE!
EE!
EE!
EE!
uh-oh...

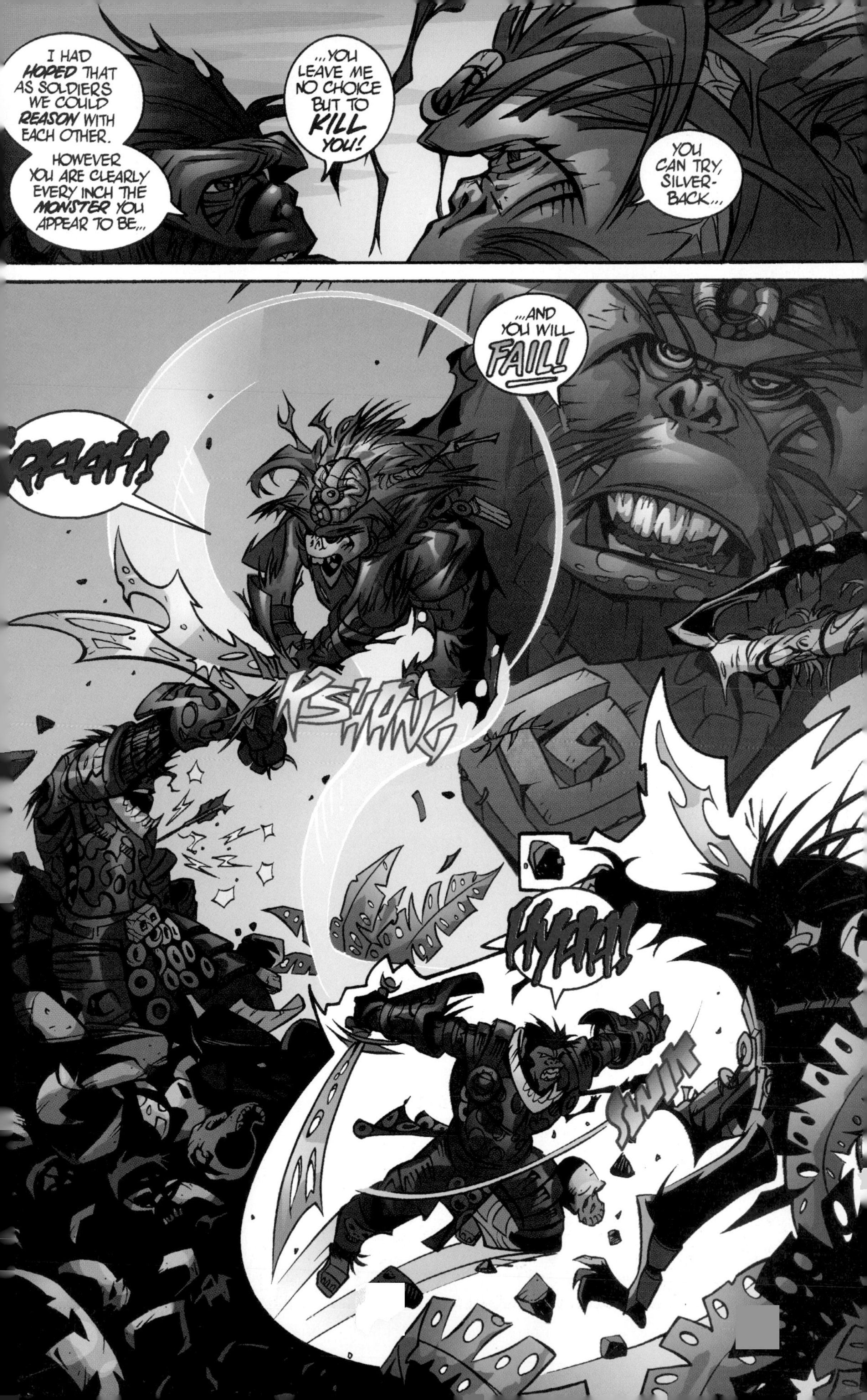
I HAD HOPED THAT AS SOLDIERS WE COULD REASON WITH EACH OTHER.
HOWEVER YOU ARE CLEARLY EVERY INCH THE MONSTER YOU APPEAR TO BE...
...YOU LEAVE ME NO CHOICE BUT TO KILL YOU!
YOU CAN TRY, SILVER-BACK...
...AND YOU WILL FAIL!
RAAAH!
KSHANK
HYAAA!
SWIIK

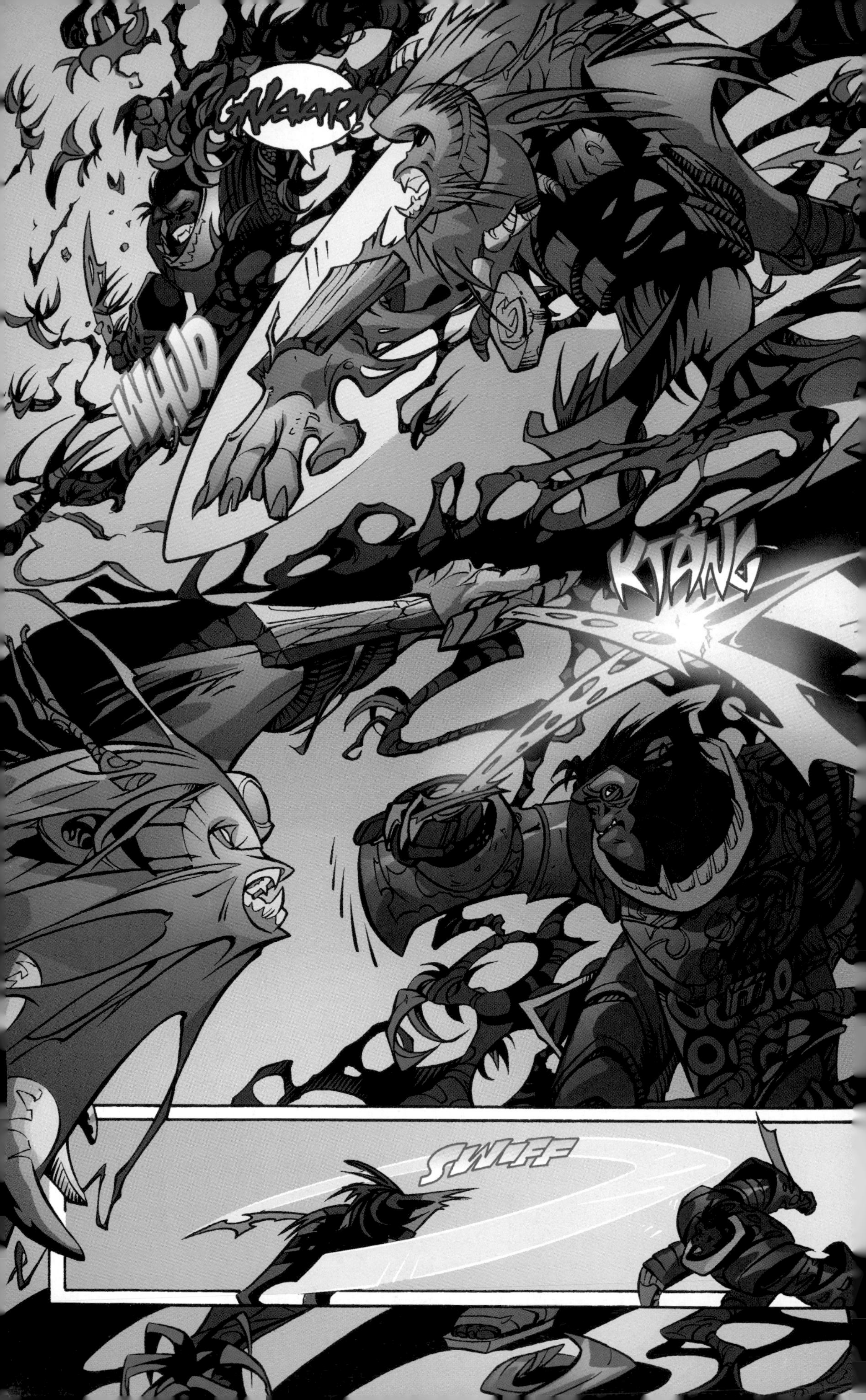
GNAAAR!
WHUD
KTANG
SWIFF

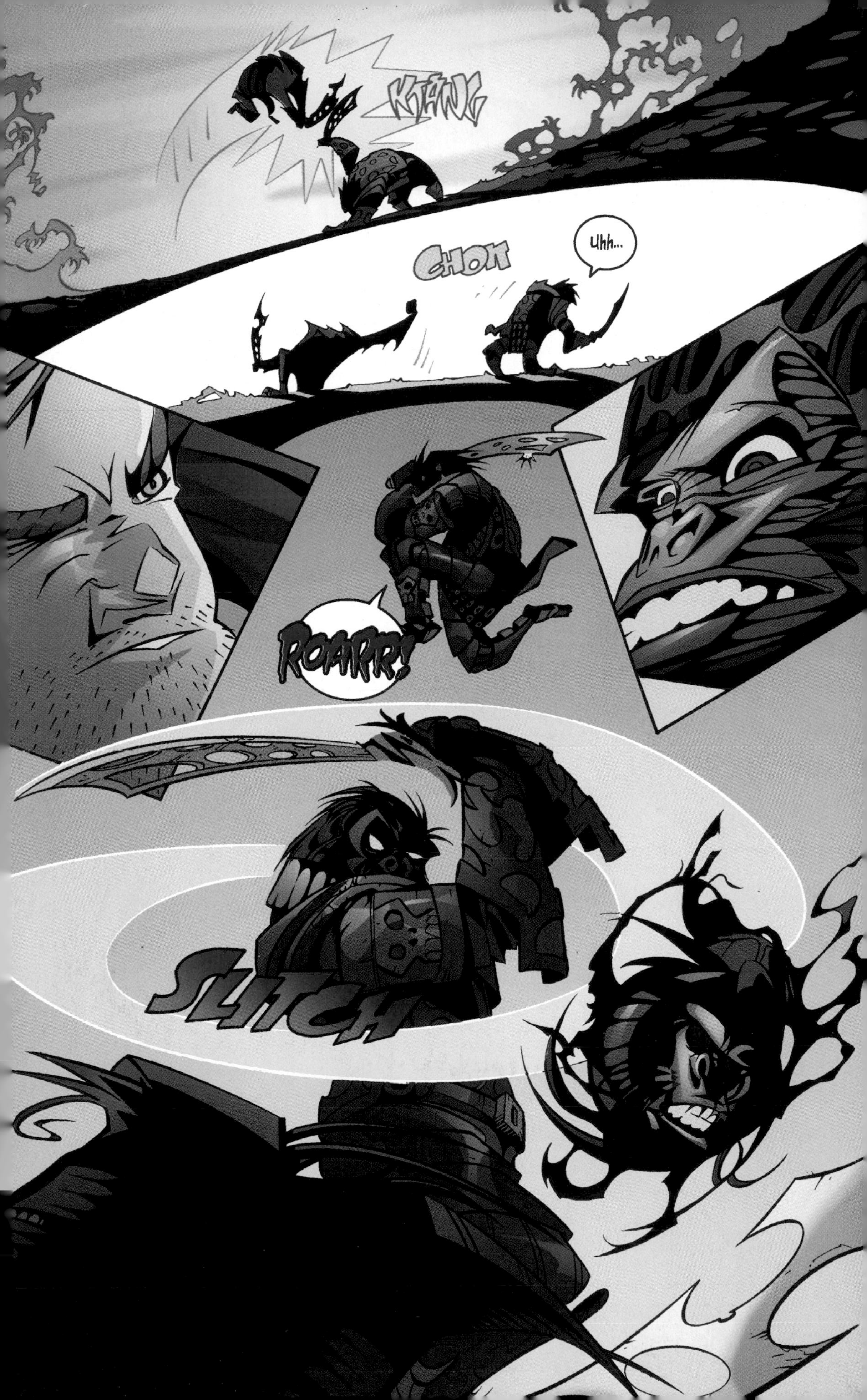
KTANG
CHOM
Uhh...
ROARR!
SLITCH

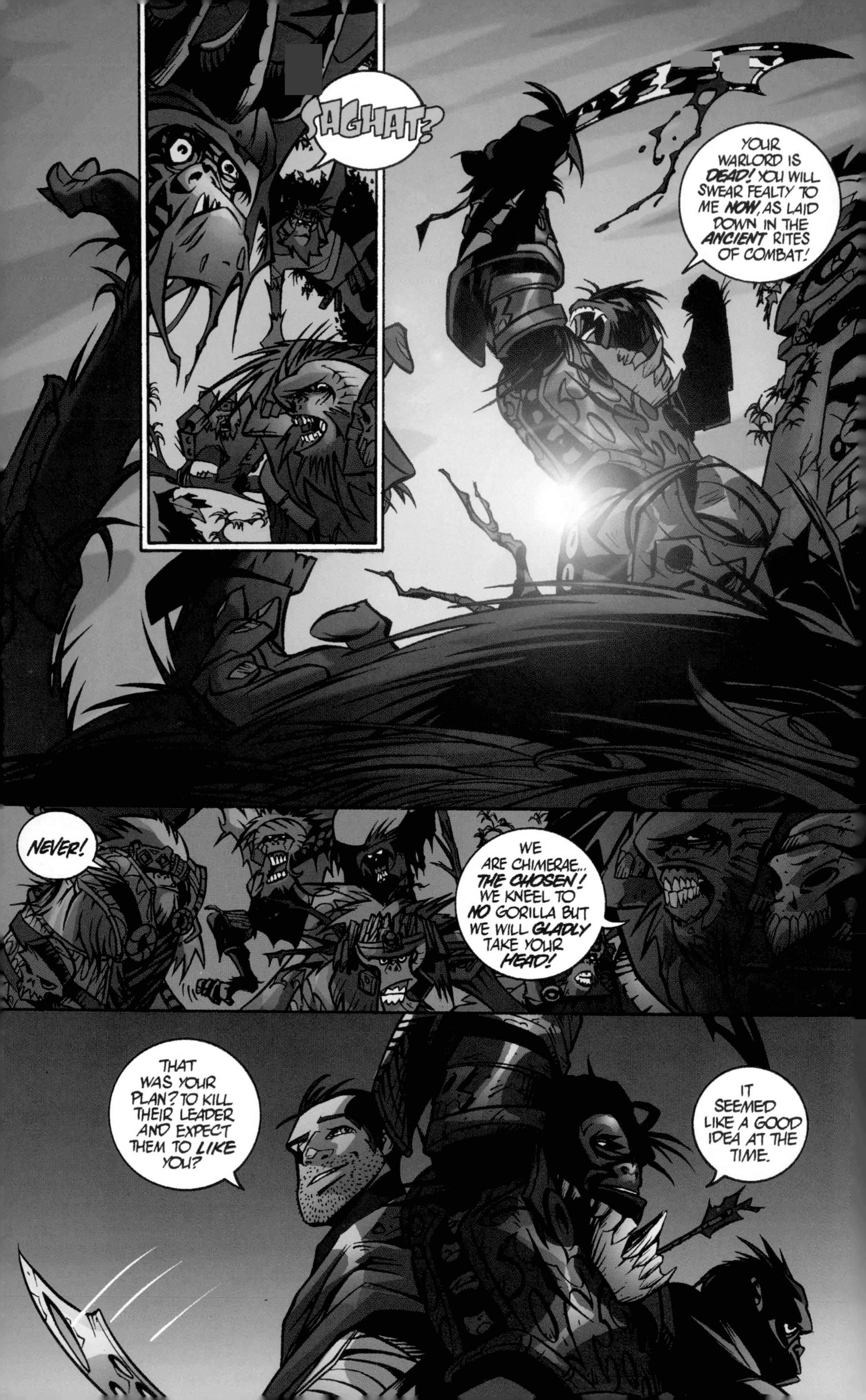
SAGHAT?
YOUR WARLORD IS DEAD! YOU WILL SWEAR FEALTY TO ME NOW, AS LAID DOWN IN THE ANCIENT RITES OF COMBAT!
NEVER!
WE ARE CHIMERAE... THE CHOSEN! WE KNEEL TO NO GORILLA BUT WE WILL GLADLY TAKE YOUR HEAD!
THAT WAS YOUR PLAN? TO KILL THEIR LEADER AND EXPECT THEM TO LIKE YOU?
IT SEEMED LIKE A GOOD IDEA AT THE TIME.

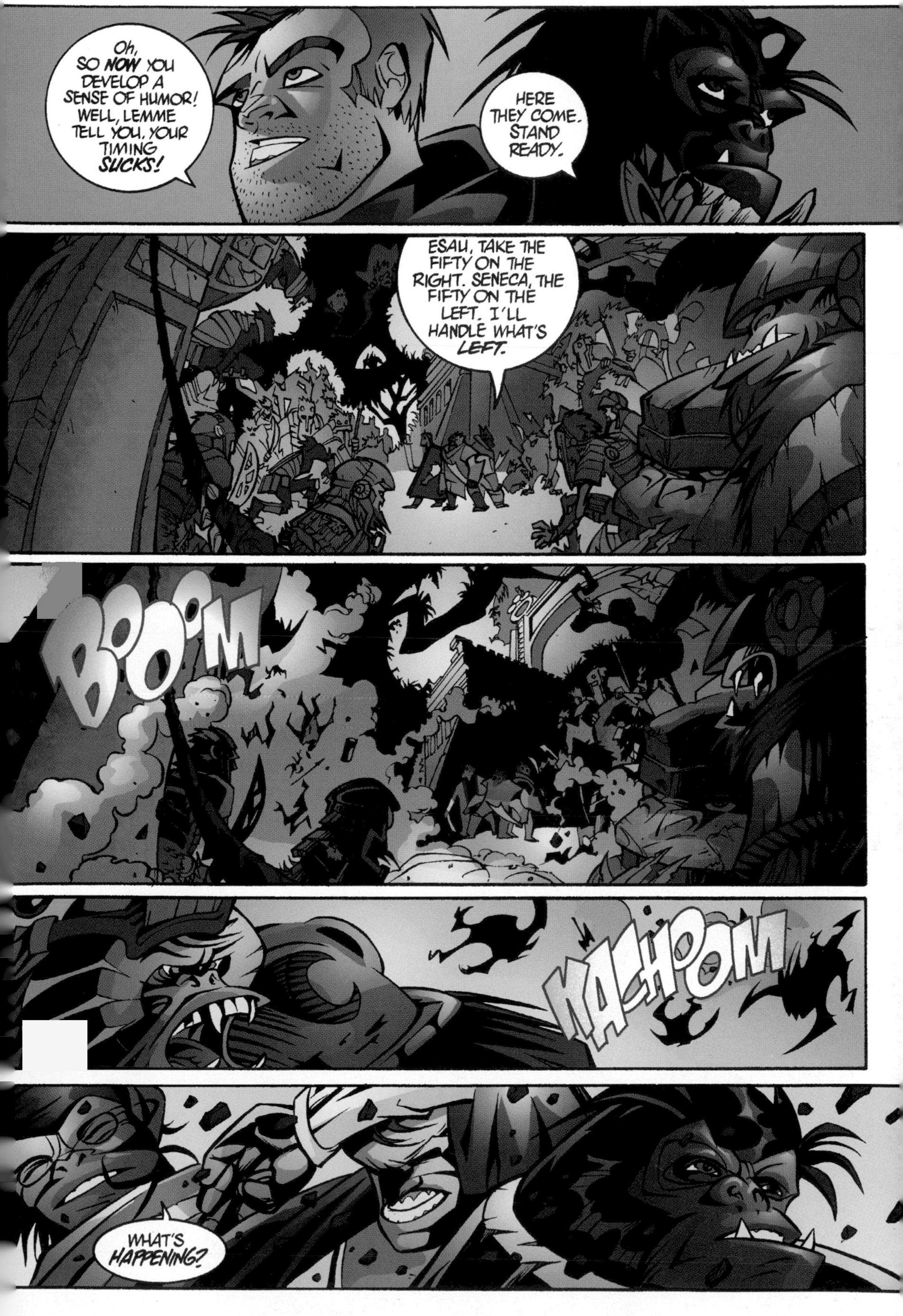
Oh, SO NOW YOU DEVELOP A SENSE OF HUMOR! WELL, LEMME TELL YOU, YOUR TIMING SUCKS!
HERE THEY COME. STAND READY.
ESAU, TAKE THE FIFTY ON THE RIGHT. SENECA, THE FIFTY ON THE LEFT. I'LL HANDLE WHAT'S LEFT.
BOOOM
KA-HOOOM
WHAT'S HAPPENING?

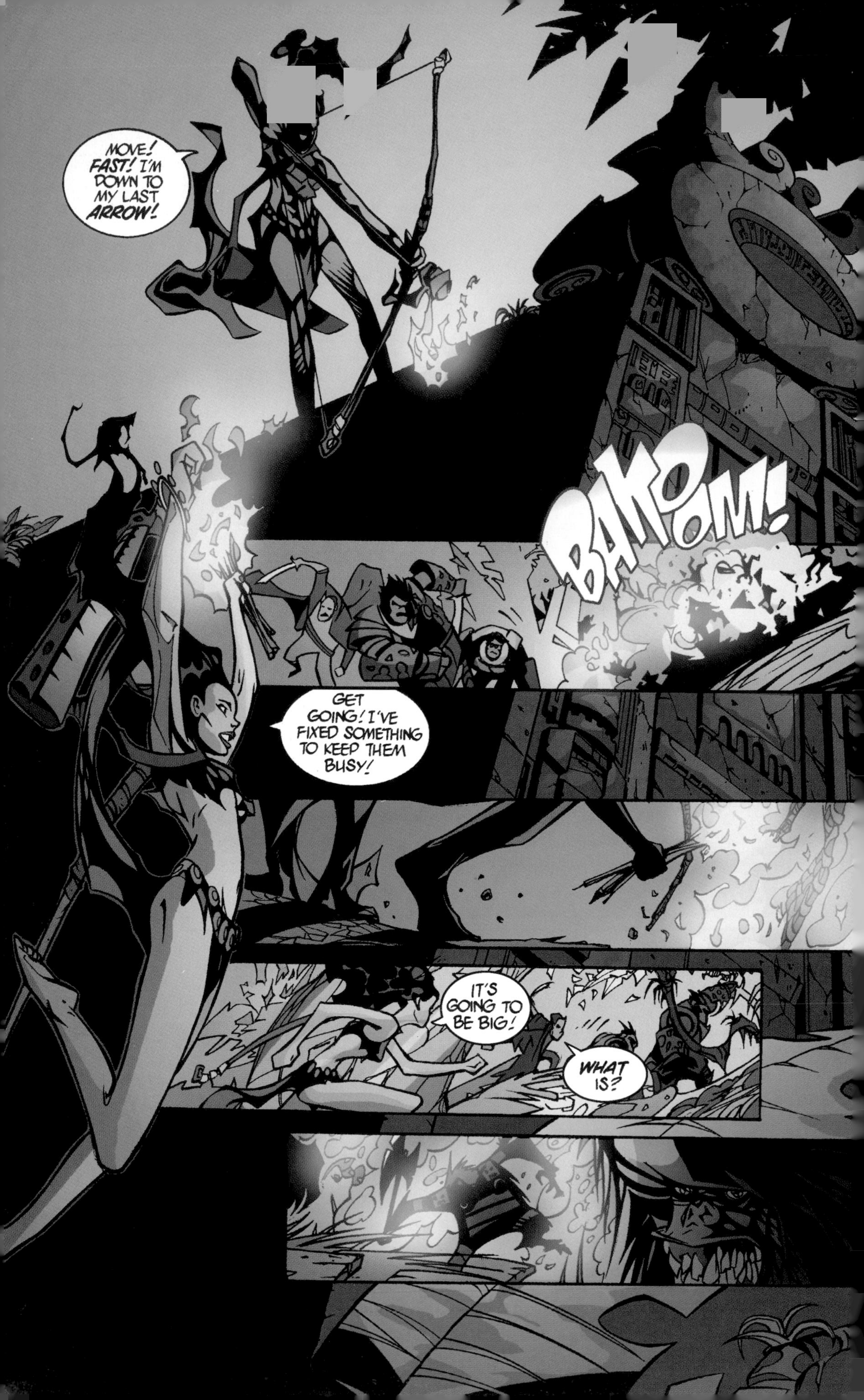
MOVE! FAST! I'M DOWN TO MY LAST ARROW!
BAROOM!
GET GOING! I'VE FIXED SOMETHING TO KEEP THEM BUSY!
IT'S GOING TO BE BIG!
WHAT IS?

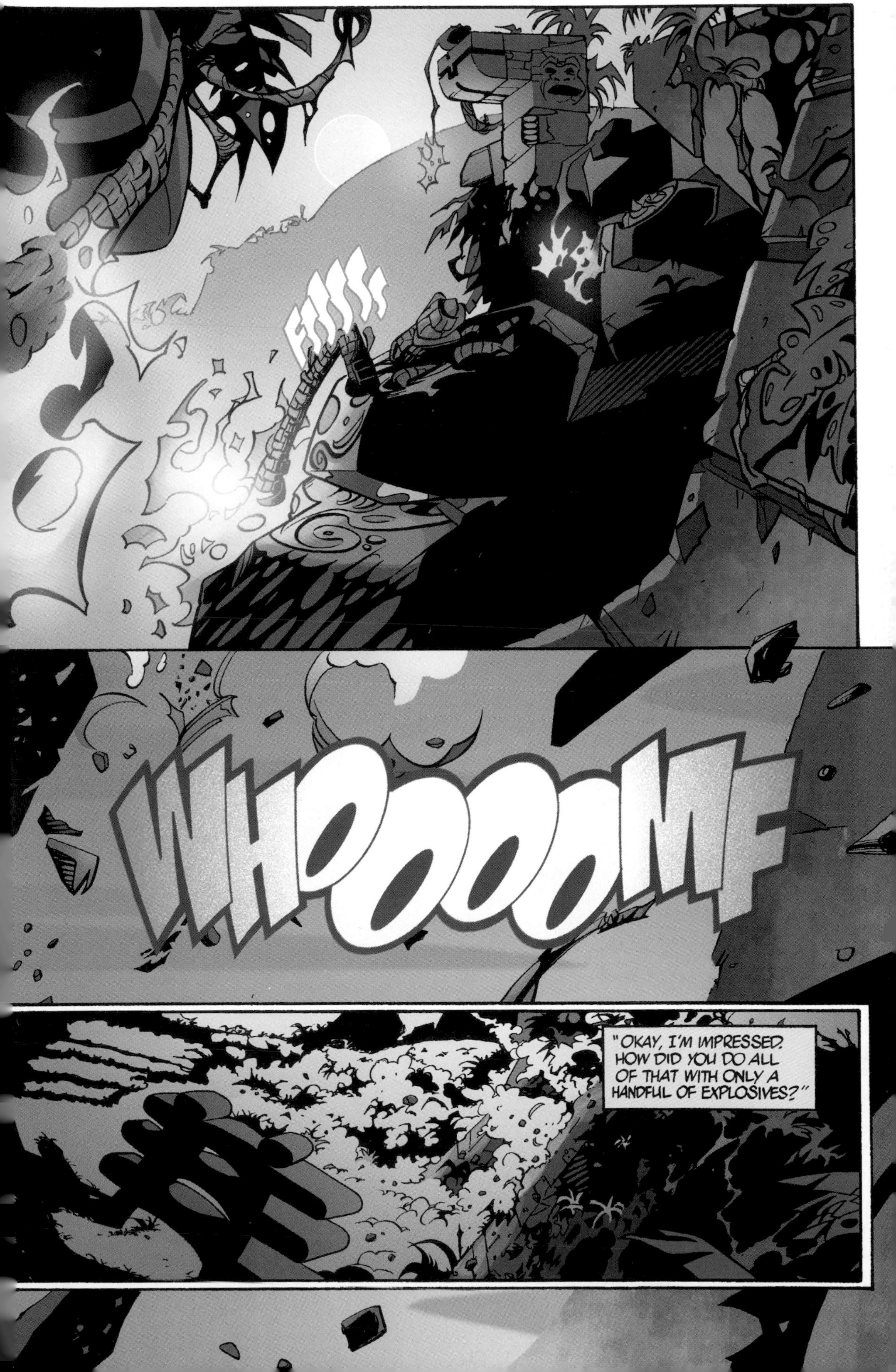
FSSSS
WHOOOOOMF
"OKAY, I'M IMPRESSED. HOW DID YOU DO ALL OF THAT WITH ONLY A HANDFUL OF EXPLOSIVES?"

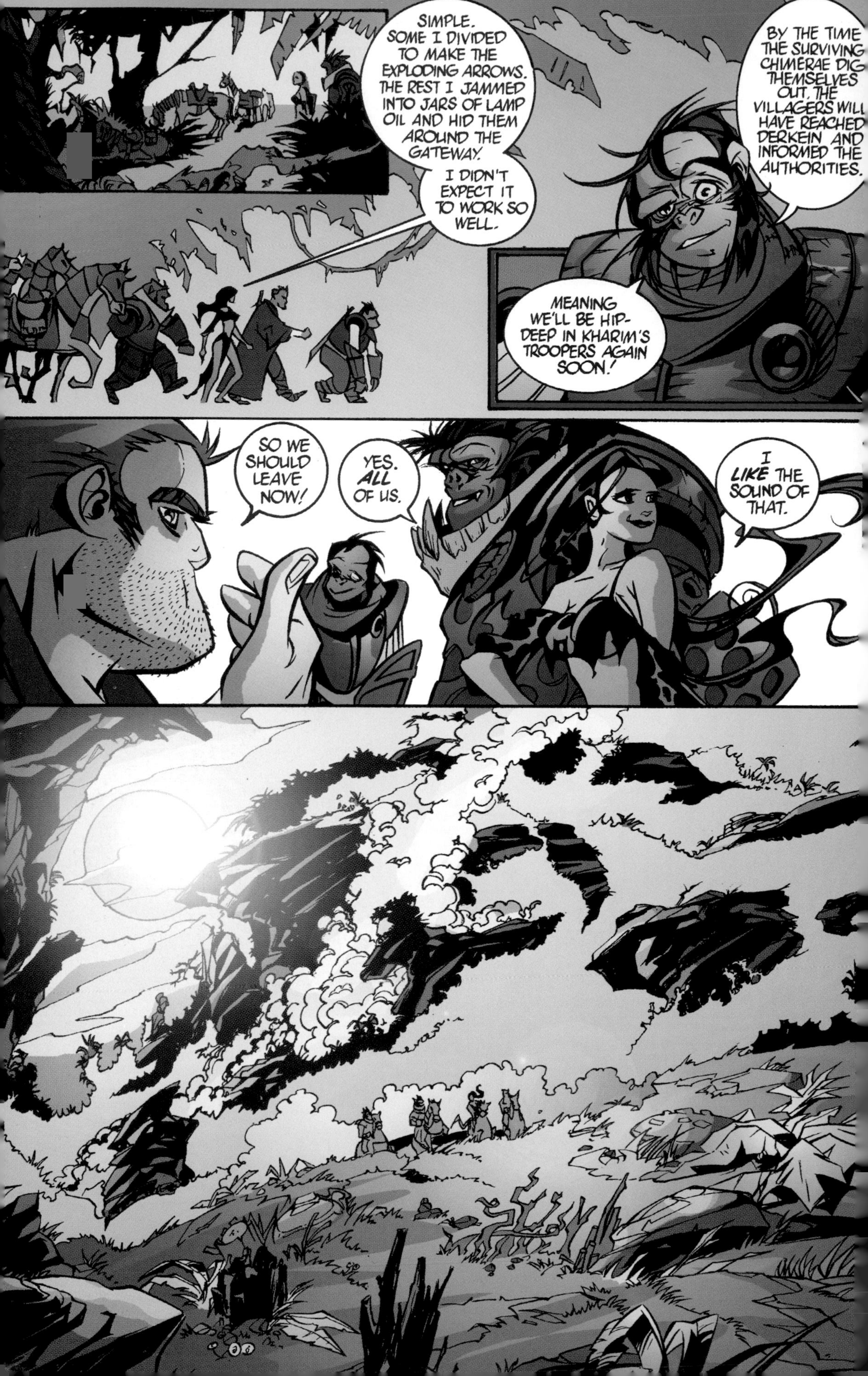
SIMPLE. SOME I DIVIDED TO MAKE THE EXPLODING ARROWS. THE REST I JAMMED INTO JARS OF LAMP OIL AND HID THEM AROUND THE GATEWAY.
I DIDN'T EXPECT IT TO WORK SO WELL.
BY THE TIME THE SURVIVING CHIMERAE DIG THEMSELVES OUT, THE VILLAGERS WILL HAVE REACHED DERKEIN AND INFORMED THE AUTHORITIES.
MEANING WE'LL BE HIP-DEEP IN KHARIM'S TROOPERS AGAIN SOON!
SO WE SHOULD LEAVE NOW!
YES. ALL OF US.
I LIKE THE SOUND OF THAT.

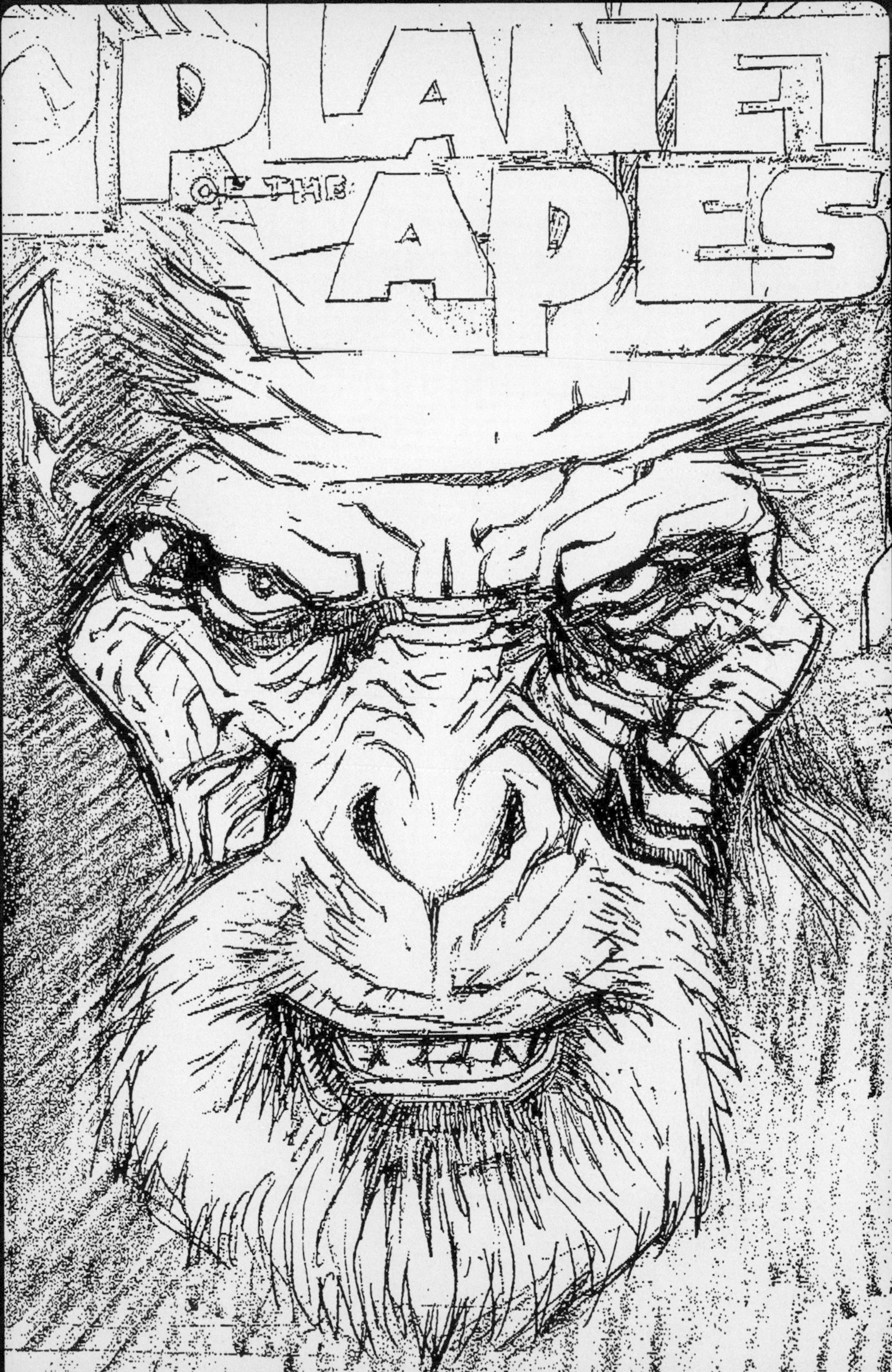
PLANET
OF THE
APES

Sketch by Derek Thompson

Gallery

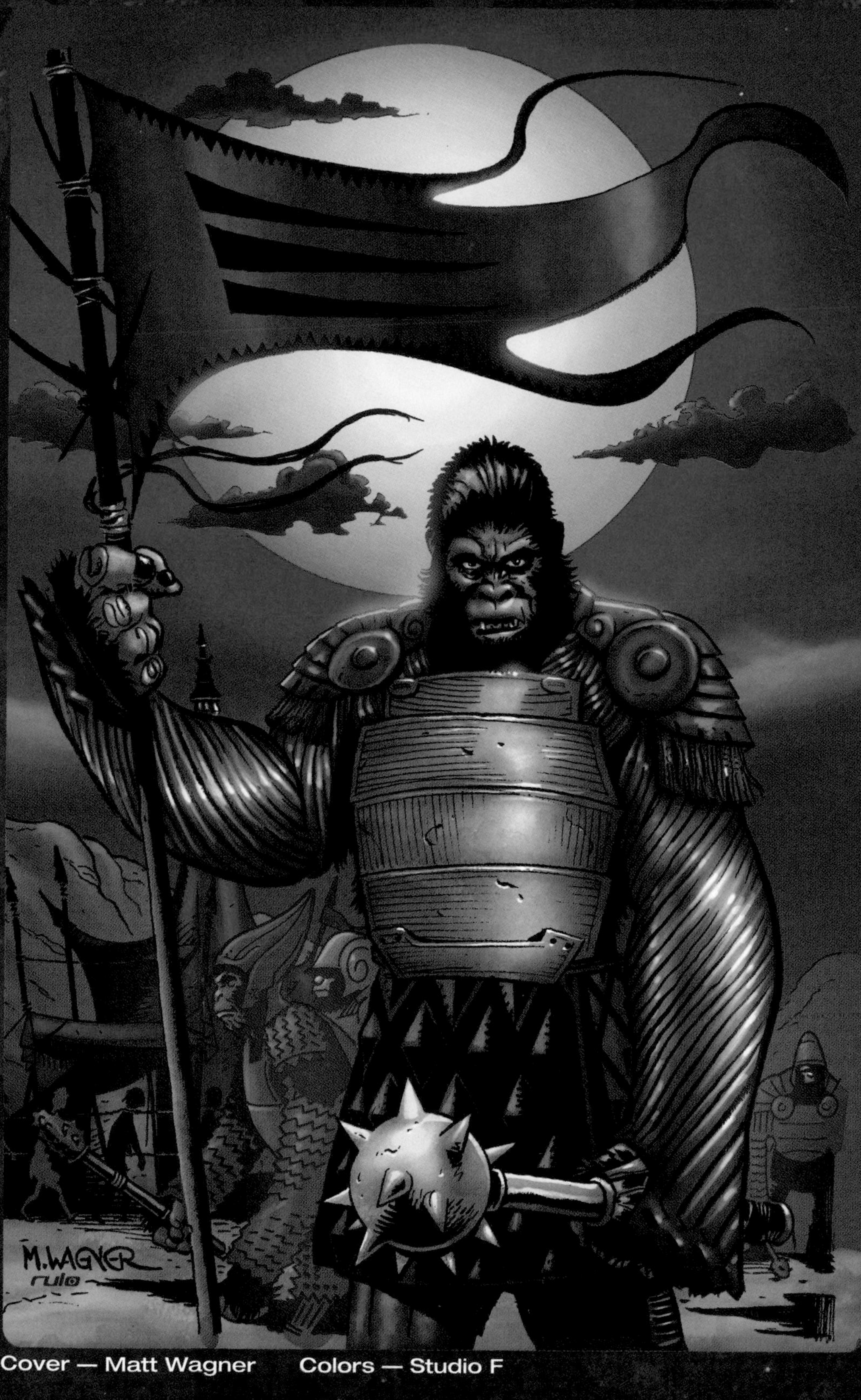
M.WAGNER
rulo
Cover — Matt Wagner Colors — Studio F

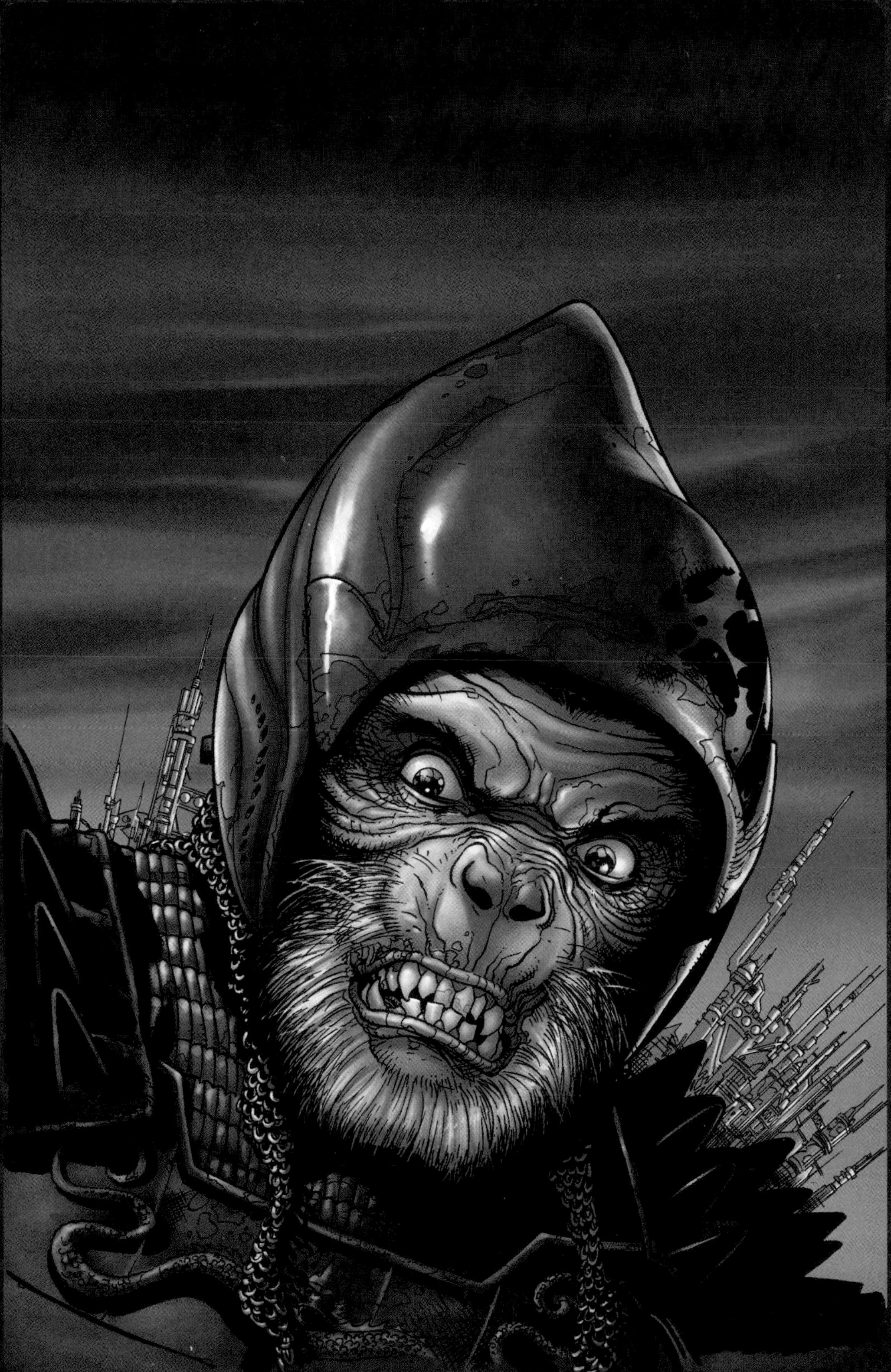

Cover — Kilian Plunkett   Colors — Studio F

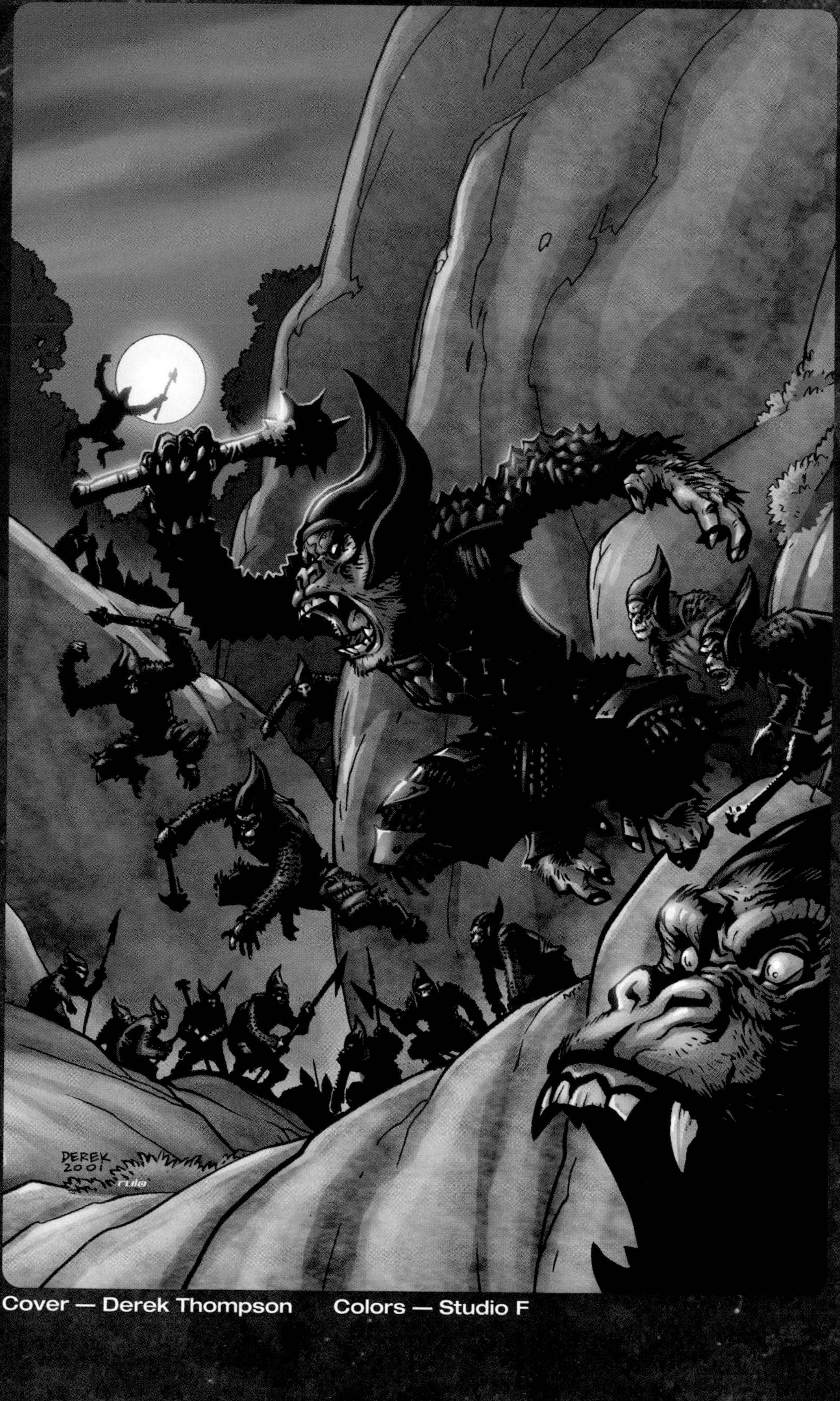
DEREK
2001
rulo
Cover — Derek Thompson   Colors — Studio F

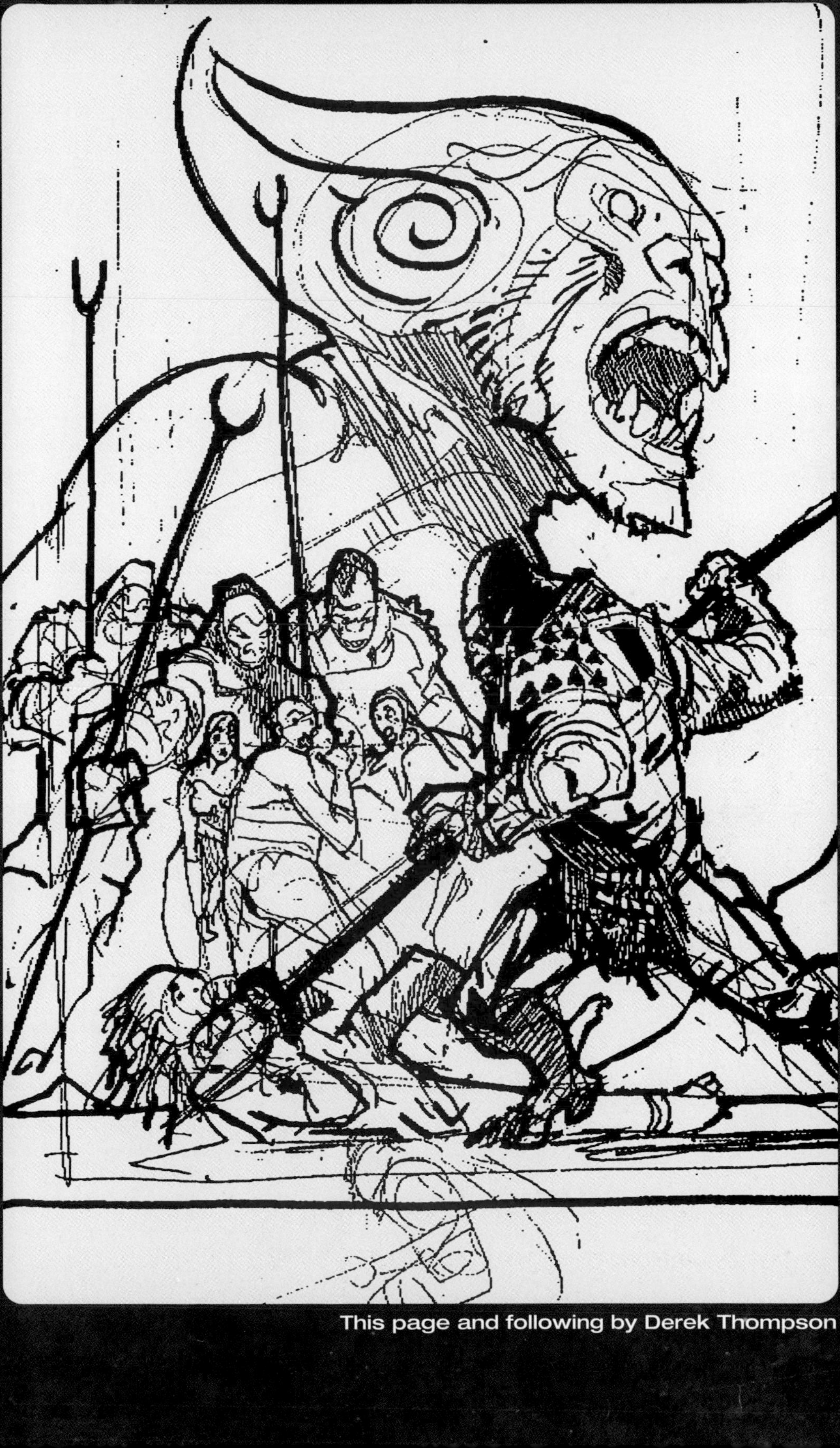

This page and following by Derek Thompson

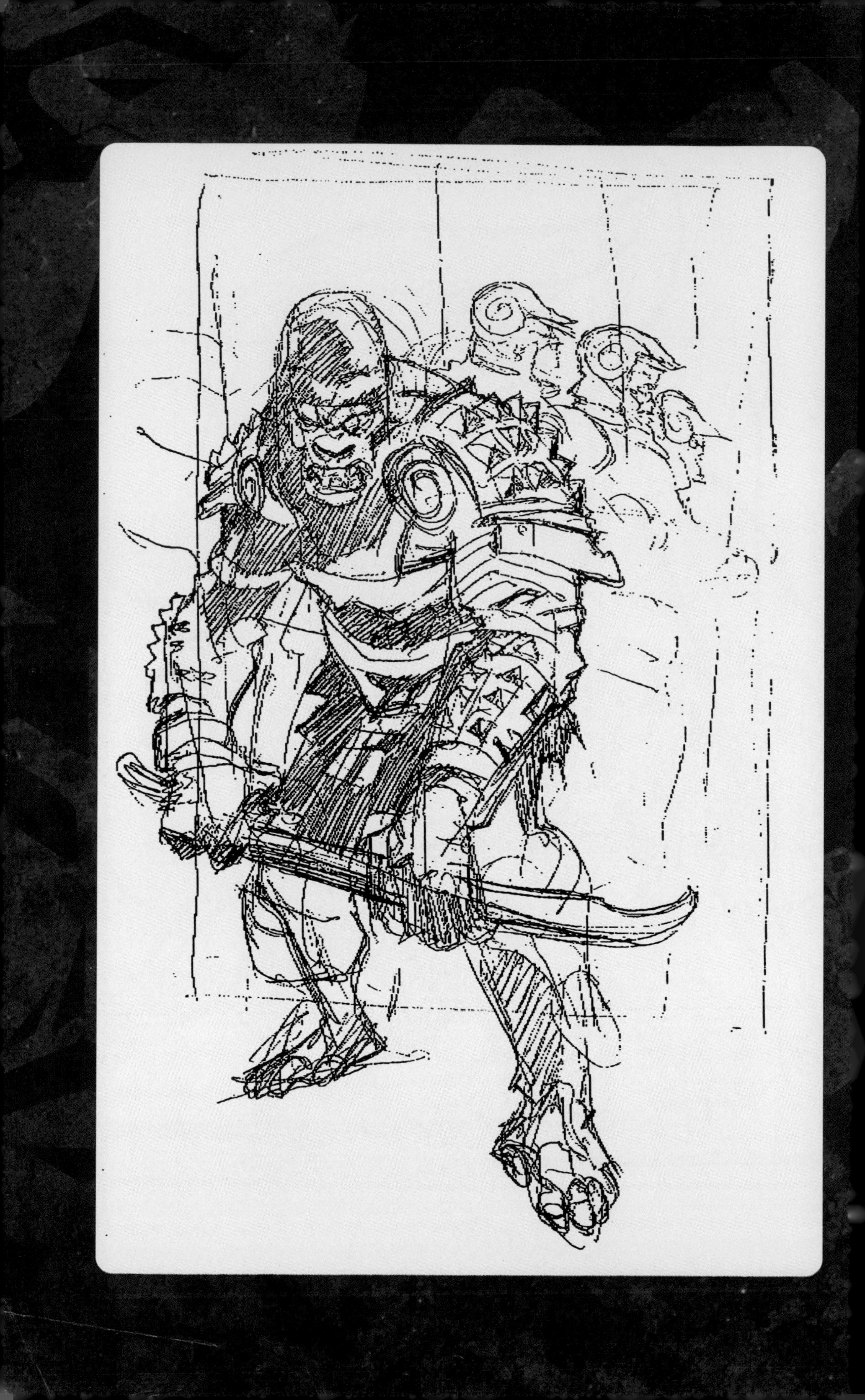

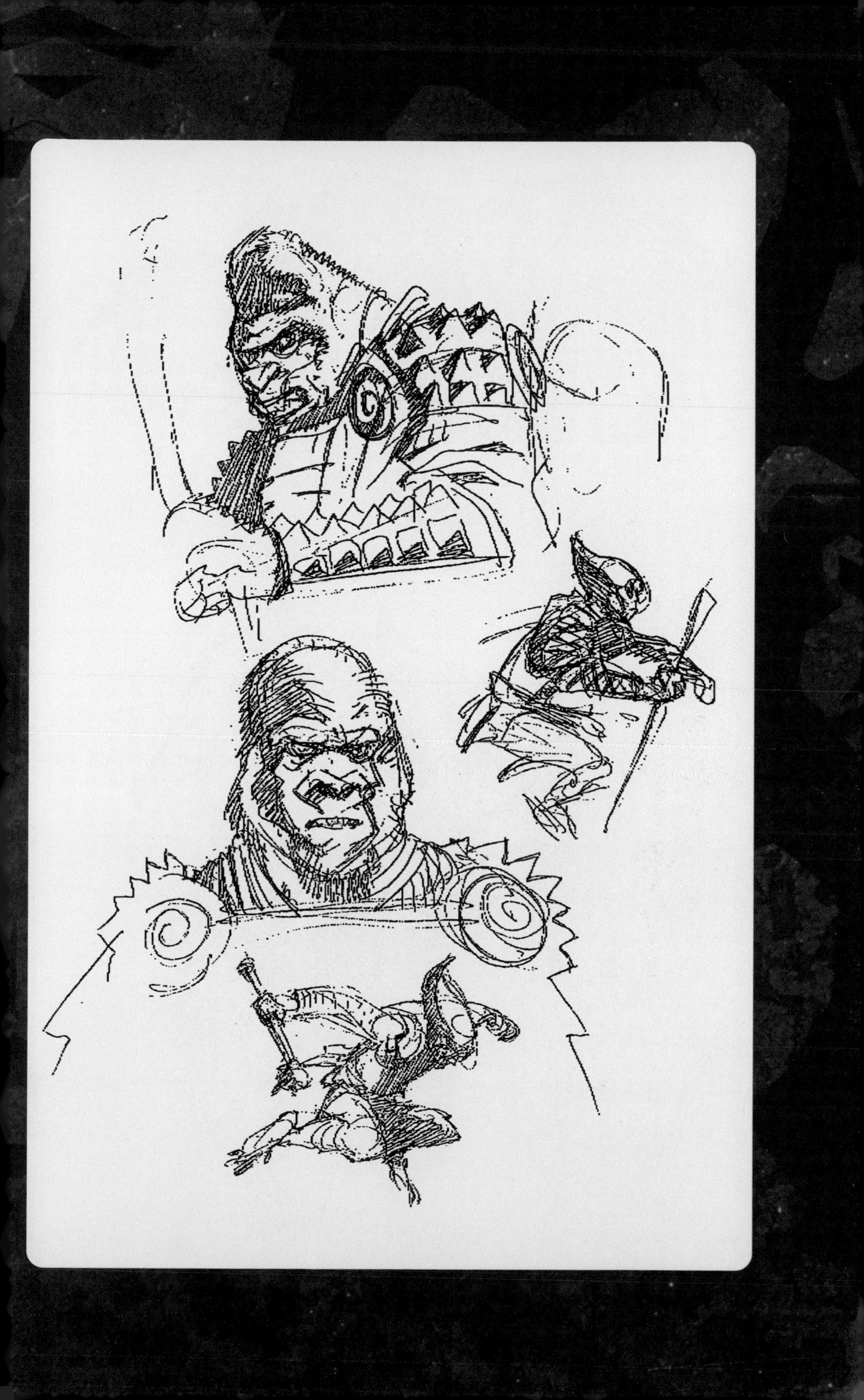

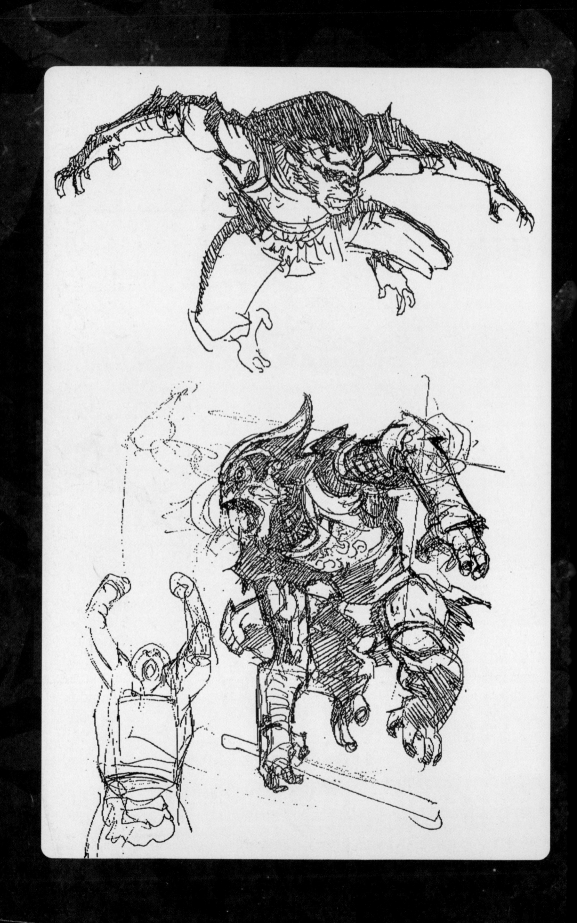

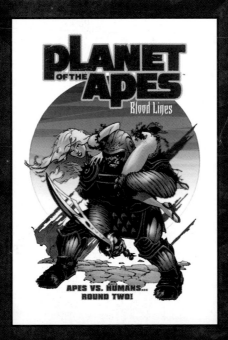

BUFFY THE VAMPIRE SLAYER™, ANGEL™, ALIENS™, AND *PREDATOR™*
TRADE PAPERBACKS AVAILABLE FROM DARK HORSE COMICS

BUFFY THE VAMPIRE SLAYER

THE DUST WALTZ
Brereton • Gomez • Florea
color paperback
ISBN: 1-56971-342-1 $9.95

THE REMAINING SUNLIGHT
Watson • Bennett • Ketcham
color paperback
ISBN: 1-56971-354-5 $9.95

THE ORIGIN
Golden • Brereton • Bennett • Ketcham
color paperback
ISBN: 1-56971-429-0 $9.95

UNINVITED GUESTS
Watson • Gomez • Florea
color paperback
ISBN: 1-56971-436-3 $10.95

SUPERNATURAL DEFENSE KIT
Watson • Richards • Pimentel
color hardcover w/slipcase
comes with golden-colored cross,
"claddagh" ring, and vial of "holy water"
ISBN: 1-56971-486-X $19.95

BAD BLOOD
Watson • Bennett • Ketcham
color paperback
ISBN: 1-56971-445-2 $9.95

CRASH TEST DEMONS
Watson • Richards • Pimentel
color paperback
ISBN: 1-56971-461-4 $9.95

RING OF FIRE
Petrie • Sook
color paperback
ISBN: 1-56971-482-7 $9.95

PALE REFLECTIONS
Watson • Richards • Pimentel
color paperback
ISBN: 1-56971-475-4 $9.95

THE BLOOD OF CARTHAGE
Golden • Richards • Pimentel
color paperback
ISBN: 1-56971-534-3 $12.95

ANGEL

THE HOLLOWER
Golden • Gomez • Florea
color paperback
ISBN: 1-56971-450-9 $9.95

SURROGATES
Golden • Zanier • Owens
color paperback
ISBN: 1-56971-491-6 $9.95

EARTHLY POSSESSIONS
Golden • Sneigoski • Zanier • Owens
color paperback
ISBN: 1-56971-533-5 $9.95

ALIENS

OUTBREAK
Verheiden • Nelson
color paperback
ISBN: 1-56971-174-7 $17.95

NIGHTMARE ASYLUM
Verheiden • Beauvais
color paperback
ISBN: 1-56971-217-4 $16.95

FEMALE WAR
Verheiden • Kieth
color paperback
ISBN: 1-56971-190-9 $16.95

GENOCIDE
Arcudi • Willis • Story
color paperback
ISBN: 1-56971-196-8 $16.95

HARVEST
Prosser • Jones
color paperback
ISBN: 1-56971-198-4 $16.95

ROGUE
Edginton • Simpson
color paperback
ISBN: 1-56971-267-0 $16.95

LABYRINTH
Woodring • Plunkett
color paperback
ISBN: 1-56971-245-X $17.95

STRONGHOLD
Arcudi • Mahnke • Palmiotti
color paperback
ISBN: 1-56971-262-X $16.95

TRIBES
Bissette • Dorman
color hardcover
ISBN: 1-878574-28-0 $24.95

KIDNAPPED
Woodring • Green • Lopez
color paperback
ISBN: 1-56971-372-3 $9.95

APOCALYPSE — THE DESTROYING ANGELS
Schultz • Wheatley
color paperback
ISBN: 1-56971-399-5 $10.95

ALIENS VS PREDATOR

ALIENS VS PREDATOR
Stradley • Norwood • Warner
color paperback
ISBN: 1-56971-125-9 $19.95

THE DEADLIEST OF THE SPECIES
Claremont • Barreto • Guice
color limited hardcover
ISBN: 1-56971-182-8 $99.95

WAR
Stradley • Saltares • Warner
color paperback
ISBN: 1-56971-158-5 $19.95

ETERNAL
Edginton • Maleev
color paperback
ISBN: 1-56971-409-6 $9.95

BATMAN/ALIENS
Marz • Wrightson
color paperback
ISBN: 1-56971-305-7 $14.95

SUPERMAN VS ALIENS
Jurgens • Nowlan
color paperback
ISBN: 1-56971-167-4 $14.95

PREDATOR

CONCRETE JUNGLE
Verheiden • Warner • Randall
color paperback
ISBN: 1-56971-165-8 $14.95

BIG GAME
Arcudi • Dorkin • Gil
color paperback
ISBN: 1-56971-166-6 $14.95

COLD WAR
Verheiden • Randall • Mitchell
color paperback
ISBN: 1-878574-79-5 $13.95

RACE WAR
Vachss • Stradley • Raskin • Pelle
color paperback
ISBN: 1-56971-112-7 $17.95

HELL & HOT WATER
Schultz • Colan
color paperback
ISBN: 1-56971-271-9 $9.95

KINDRED
Lamb • Tolson • O'Connell • Peterson
color paperback
ISBN: 1-56971-270-0 $14.95

PREDATOR VS JUDGE DREDD
Wagner • Alcatena
color paperback
ISBN: 1-56971-345-6 $9.95

TARZAN VS PREDATOR AT THE EARTH'S CORE
Simonson • Weeks
color paperback
ISBN: 1-56971-231-X $12.95

Available from your local comics shop or bookstore!

To find a comics shop in your area, call 1-888-266-4226
For more information or to order direct:
•On the web: www.darkhorse.com •E-mail: mailorder@darkhorse.com
•Phone: 1-800-862-0052 or (503) 652-9701 Mon.-Sat. 9 A.M. to 5 P.M. Pacific Time
*Prices and availability subject to change without notice